SAVE ME!

SAVE ME!

A Young Woman's Journey
Through Schizophrenia to Health

JUDY LEE

A DOUBLEDAY-GALILEE ORIGINAL

DOUBLEDAY & COMPANY, INC., GARDEN CITY, NEW YORK 1980

Library of Congress Cataloging in Publication Data

Lee, Judy.
  Save me!

  "A Doubleday-Galilee original."
    1. Lee, Judy.   2. Christian biography—United States.   3. Schizo-
phrenia—Biography.   I. Title.
BR1725.L34A35   248'.86 [B]
ISBN: 0-385-15101-2
Library of Congress Catalog Card Number 78-22365

Contents

Introduction

"You have good reason to have gone over the deep end. But, you have no reason to stay there forever." This statement by one of Judy Lee's therapists rings true to all of the best that psychotherapy has to offer. It combines reality and yet hope. It offers freedom from guilt, yet not refuge from responsibility and growth. In a similar way *Save Me!* is a book which maintains balance throughout its pages both spiritually and psychologically.

Spiritually there is a ring of honesty as Christians are presented varyingly, from accepting to critical, loving to selfish. Traditional Christian thinking is portrayed well—the questioning of Judy's going to a non-Christian therapist and the overspiritualizing of her psychological needs. Real gut Christianity in the truest biblical sense is shown in the love and consistent support of some of her Christian friends. Above all, the unavoidable evidence of Divine intervention in her life in a miraculous fashion portrays the God of the Bible as being just as real and active today as He ever was in ancient times. Those in the church who dispute the fact of a miraculous God will find this book a challenge to reckon with.

Psychologically there is equal balance and honesty. Labels and tags are shown for all of their destructiveness in making people feel hopeless and stigmatized. Yet the same professionals who hurt people with these labels are portrayed as so often they really are, kind and caring but misinformed and helpless. They are not evil and cold as so often Christians feel they are.

Schizophrenia—that misunderstood, often vague term which by its very name frightens so many—is presented with hope. In her honesty Judy Lee skillfully shows its pain as well as its potential cure. And hope for schizophrenics is a quality which has been long needed in the psychological field as well as among Christians.

With a breath of fresh air Reality Therapy is presented as an adjunct to Judy's fast-growing Christian faith. Her therapy here particularly shows the lack of antagonism which can exist between psychotherapy and the Christian faith. In a perfect balance there is psychotherapy, Christian faith, and the Divine Miracle.

Save Me! would be a help to not only the layman who has problems or helps those with problems—but the professional in the field who wants to expand his base of expertise. The reader who pursues these thoughts with balance, realizing that each man must carve out his own solutions in his own way, will find in this book a myriad of possible avenues of answers for an age-old problem—the problem of mental illness.

ELIZABETH SKOGLUND

Editor's Note

To protect the privacy of the individuals involved in Judy's life story, all names in her book have been changed. People and places have been disguised so as not to be recognizable, but her story remains true; her healing remains a reality.

SAVE ME!

1 Broken

My psychiatrist, Dr. Dane, leaned over and looked me straight in the eyes. "Judy," he said, "you are a paranoid schizophrenic. I don't know what your chances are for recovery. We're not sure why. . . ." I hung my head.

I remembered the months before when I'd asked why there were no answers—why there was nothing to hold onto. I had searched everywhere for truth and left no stone unturned. I had tried everything the world had to offer. There was, for me, no satisfaction in people or things. The world had become a stinking pit of lies and deception. I had nowhere to turn.

So I began to deny reality. I started to wipe out my own existence, my friends, my family, and my school. And as I denied their existence I began to lose my grip. What was—and what was not—happening became unclear to me. I could not discern between the real and the unreal. I was hanging between two worlds.

Looking for a realm which confirmed my existence, I found that my life did not really matter. I could not live in a world which was unconcerned about me. So, over a matter of time, I created another world in my mind—a place where nothing mattered and everything was as unimportant as I.

This world resembled a vacuum. There was a total absence of

love and joy. Anything of value could not come into this realm, as it was a place where all things were valueless.

But, it offered quiet from the lies around me and peace in exchange for the constant questions that tumbled through my mind. Here there were no questions because they had all been answered in one sentence, "Nothing is real."

At first, I could come and go as I pleased from my world. I could choose when I did—and did not—want to be there. But the more time I spent there, the more tempting it became never to "go back." And I struggled for hours at a time as to where I wanted to be. I had a choice to make which I could tell no one about. If I "left," I decided that I would never come back—unless I found something to live for.

I knew that no one would understand where I was going. I had told no one of the world I had found, because I didn't want anyone to try to hold me back. I believed I had found another realm which anyone could cross into if they wished. But I knew that only I had the key to the door. And I wasn't going to let anyone in.

One evening, while I was sitting in my college dorm room, I decided to "leave." I sat on my bed and set my mind on the other world. Slowly, the door opened for me. I ran across the threshold and slammed and locked the door. But after I locked it, I realized that I did not have the strength to get out. I had lost the will to fight for my life.

"Judy!!" Dr. Dane yelled, trying to get my attention.

I lifted my head, tears streaming down my face. I was trying to listen but I'd missed several minutes of his conversation with me. It was so hard to stay in "his" world and not slip back into mine.

"Judy, I'm going to put you on medication. It will help you handle your thoughts and maybe make it a little easier for you. It will control. . . ."

I drifted back.

"I have to kill myself." I headed to my dresser, taking out a bottle of Valium I had saved.

My roommate, Kathy, and her boy friend, Joe, were at a birthday party. I was supposed to be following close behind. Instead, I opened the bottle and started swallowing the Valiums by the tens.

I sat on the edge of my bed and began to write my good-bye letter. I was angry at everyone, for no one had given me a reason to live, or a purpose to go on. I was especially angry at Ed, a new friend, because he had refused to return the love I felt for him. I didn't know why.

I finished my letter and lay down to finish the pills and die. Minutes ticked by and I could feel myself falling off. "It is finally over," I thought. And I closed my eyes, sensing how easy it was to die.

"JUDY!!" This time Dr. Dane yelled loudly to snap me back. "I'm not going to put you away in a hospital. I want to help you stay alive."

"Alive? I'm not alive," I thought as I lay in the hospital bed. Tubes were running down my nose into my stomach. "WHY am I alive, WHY??"

I started to pull the tubes out of my nose. I could feel them coming up my throat. A nurse ran in to stop me and I flung my fist as hard as I could into her stomach.

Morning. A doctor stood over me. "Judy, you have to see a psychiatrist," he said.

I looked at Dr. Dane. "Do you mean that? Can I really stay in school with my friends?"

"I think you'd do better on the outside. We'll take it a month at a time. If you reach the point where you feel you must take your life, we'll have to put you in State. But it would only be for a while."

"What about the blackouts?" I'd been plagued with memory blackouts the past few weeks. Some days, for hours at a time, I would be unable to remember where I'd been or what I'd done. And some days I would wake up in the morning and, looking in the mirror, could not remember my name or where I was.

"The medication will help that. It should control your

thoughts. I believe you have a chemical imbalance in your tempo-
ral lobe. This means that messages coming into your brain become scrambled and end up sounding like total confusion to you.
There's no way to cure it. We can only try to control it. But,
we're not even sure about that."

I looked at him, searching for hope in his eyes. I wanted to believe what he said. I wanted to hope. . . .

I walked home that evening, with no hope of healing or recovery from my illness. I lay on my bunk bed, staring at the wall, wondering how I could hold on. I believed that there was no one to
help me. "I will be like this for the rest of my life," I thought. And
tears streamed down my face because my life had been taken away
from me.

The next morning I headed to the student lounge, my local
hangout. I sat down, in a grouping of chairs, by myself. Being
alone, away from people and the struggles of day-to-day life gave
me a small sense of peace. Nothing to think about, no battles to
fight.

A woman cautiously entered my presence and sat down beside
me. She pulled a small booklet out of her pocket and asked me if
she could share with me something that meant a great deal to her.

I looked at her. Her eyes were so sincere and full of light. As I
stumbled to say no, she began to share the Gospel with me.

"God loves you and has a wonderful plan for your life," she
said. This I found totally unbelievable. "But we are separated
from God because of our sins. . . ." She showed me a picture of a
large gulf between two cliffs. I was not impressed.

"But Christ bridged the gap between God and us, in that He
died for our sins so that through Him we could know God. . . ."
she continued.

"If you confess your sins and ask Christ to come into your
heart, you can know God personally."

I looked at her as if she was completely crazy.

"Would you like that?" she asked.

Now I knew she was nuts. "No!" I said. "That is not what I
want."

She wrote her name, address, and phone number on the booklet and handed it to me as she rose to leave. "If you have any questions, please call me," she added.

I sat in shock as she left, for I was ill prepared to consider such a claim. Christ—the son of God? ALIVE TODAY? Hadn't he just died on the cross and been buried somewhere, never to be seen again?

I returned to my room, thinking about Jesus. Maybe He really was alive. Maybe He could help me, although no one else had been able to. Maybe He had an answer for me. I wasn't sure of the question.

I climbed into bed and pulled the covers over my head.

"Jesus," I said. "If you're really out there somewhere and if you're really alive, please listen to me. I've made an awful mess out of my life. Will you help me put it back together?"

As I closed my eyes and thought about the things I had just said, my mind began to wander back to the time when I was a very small child.

2 The Least of These

The town that I call home is located in the southern part of West Virginia. Located at the base of a steep mountain that attracted back-packers and campers, this small tourist town is known for its beauty and tranquility. Many campers returned year after year to spend their days beneath the pine and spruce trees that enveloped Henderson, the local state park.

My house was nestled in the woods on what was once an Indian reservation. Located at the foot of the mountain, it was spotted with pine trees and wood ferns. Many years before, all the remnants of Indian occupation had been destroyed as new houses were built to take their place. Our street was part of the "good" section of town where many of the more affluent natives settled their families.

I was born the fourth and last child of respected, well-established parents. My roots on my mother's side stemmed back to the earliest settlers of America. Her ancestors' names are found in some of the oldest cemeteries in this country and many of the historical accounts of the settling of America. I wasn't told this until I was twenty-two.

My father's side is mostly English. My great-grandfather had immigrated many years before from England. He died when I was a small child, but I shall never forget his old rustic house with a hand pump in the kitchen sink. There was a special place in my heart for this part of my heritage. It was the only exposure I had to really belonging somewhere. I grew up being proud of being of English descent.

I have two sisters and a brother. My sister Anne, the oldest, is nine years my senior and has always been a stranger to me. The years between us kept us distant, and I have never been able to bridge the gap. Frank, my only brother, is four years older than I. Although we were never close in words or emotions, I have felt him to be the most special person in the family. We have never needed words, for he has always understood the expression on my face and the look in my eyes. Phyllis, separated from me by only two years, was my best buddy and friend all throughout my childhood. My mother dressed us like twins and there was little that we didn't share. We were inseparable partners.

We were not a close-knit family. My mother spent much of her time trying to hold us all together and give us a sense of family. It was she who made Christmas an exciting event. She had a way of throwing her whole self into our games and outings which made them fun and sometimes even tolerable. Without her, we would have been nothing.

There were relatives on both sides of the family who came from Boston, Chicago, and Tennessee to share Thanksgiving dinner, Easter vacation, and summer fun. Since they were seldom around, I could not see how they fit into my life at all. Aunts, uncles, grandparents, and cousins were unable to hold my interest, for I cared little for them. They may have sensed my lack of love, because I became known as the family brat. It was not uncommon for an aunt or uncle to take me aside and spank me for some childish prank. So I grew up fearing the times when they would come to visit. I was especially leery of what they thought of me. I had a great sense of dignity that they seemed to wipe out upon arrival.

Life, as the youngest child, was filled with exclusion from many activities. I was always too young, too small, or too dumb to do the things that my sisters and brother did. It is not surprising, then, that my two earliest memories are that of being locked in the kitchen while everyone else went outside to play baseball, and standing alone on the street corner as Phyllis left on a bus for kindergarten. I hated being the "baby" of the family and having my cheeks pinched.

In my loneliness I created an imaginary friend named Candy. While the rest of the world was occupied with things I couldn't do, I would walk down the street to his house. Candy lived in a large Colonial house that overlooked the entrance to the "reservation." We spent two years together, playing games and singing songs.

My mother, quite pleased that I was pleasantly occupied, never discouraged me from seeing him. She sensed my loneliness and knew that one day I would outgrow his company. Some days she would ask me what Candy and I had done—listening intently to my stories of adventure.

I did outgrow Candy as I entered the Sunday school at the local Baptist church and learned about angels. My teacher told me that they did exist and I had no cause to doubt her word. The first Sunday I heard this great news I planned my strategy for making contact with them.

I decided that the perfect place was in my front yard. So I would go sit on my front stoop and begin to talk with them. I knew I could tell them anything I wanted and that they would listen. On days when I was extremely happy, I would ask them to hold my hands as we danced around the yard in a circle.

On really dull days we would take jaunts into the woods. This was a very joyful time for me, because I could explain all the high points of nature and show off my superior knowledge. Hiking through bushes, briars and trees, I would tell them the story of the wood flowers—how they came to be what they were and why. Very politely, my angels would listen and follow me every step of the way. Yet I was the only one who came home dirty from head to toe, as the angels always remained white and clean in their long, flowing gowns.

My preoccupation with angels was interrupted by my mother's insistence that I take piano lessons. Her aunt, I was told, was a great pianist and it was decided that my talent was no less than hers. I would, of course, be a superstar, and I had to start immediately.

Mrs. Bixby, a local instructor who was known as the best in the area, was hired to teach me all she knew. And once a week I was shipped to her house to bang out chords and scales—which later evolved into memorizing long classical pieces that I played at her piano recitals.

I was thoroughly convinced that Mrs. Bixby was a full-blooded witch. Every time I made a mistake she would scream and make me start over. This caused great floods of tears, and she refused me Kleenex to wipe them away. So, each week, I stuffed my pockets with tissues and headed to her home with fear and trembling.

Mrs. Bixby lived only a bike ride away, in an older section of town. Sometimes I would ride past her house and pray that a flood from the spring thaw would rush down and wash away her house. For safety, I added the request that she be home when it happened. And every spring I waited for my prayer to be answered.

In rebellion against what I thought was her hatred for children, I practiced as little as possible—hoping that she would become discouraged and drop me. But she was as thoroughly convinced that I had talent, as was my mother—so she overlooked my negligence, tears, and dirty looks. I was drilled and drilled until I dreamed of chords. She hammered me until I could play, by memory, ten- and fifteen-page classical pieces. Having accomplished that, she signed me up for the National Piano Auditions that were graded by big-time piano teachers. But the rewards of a 96 or 98 per cent were few. I had no plans for ever becoming a great concert pianist. I was unimpressed by my talent and I thought it only natural that I should cheer when Mrs. Bixby was killed in a car crash. I was disappointed that my request for a flood had been overruled. But the day I heard the news of her death I closed the piano and felt, for the first time in years, that I was free.

Winter and early spring vacations were spent with my family in our Winnebago—traveling down the East Coast and finally parking in Florida camping grounds. After a profitable business venture, my father had bought the camper, fulfilling his lifelong dream of traveling and investigating all the hot spots of America. After a few trips, I developed a sense of "belonging on the road." I recognized all the highways and familiar sights and road signs along the way and often kept a notebook, writing in the date and time we passed these roadmarks.

Family life centered around traveling, and our traveling was centered around my father's business. My father was a real estate broker who bought large plots of land in the surrounding states to resell to investors. If he had to travel on a weekend, I could sometimes talk him into letting me go with him. Often he mixed business with pleasure and we would stop, during family trips, to look over what seemed to us masses of land. We kids spent many hours in the Winnebago as he talked through business deals in towns along our route.

I never wanted to leave this life, built around the road. I loved the people we met in restaurants and stops along the way. There was something about riding and watching the world go by that gave me a sense of power. It was exciting and I never wanted the road to end.

But there were days and weeks when I was grounded at home. I occupied my time playing baseball and football with the guys I knew. My buddy, George, who lived across the street would call me every time a game was scheduled. And I'd grab my brother's mitt and bat as I ran out the door. I was "one of the boys," a very special privilege in my neighborhood. While the girls I knew were playing dolls and silly games, I was climbing trees, building tree forts, fighting dirt-bomb wars, and getting dirty. All I did centered around being outside, although I often stayed in to play with my sister Phyllis. She was very feminine and fragile and did all the things little girls did.

I accepted school as a part of life, and even discovered that it could be fun. It was even more exciting when I found out that I was intelligent. It was nothing for me to be running neck-and-neck with the girl who eventually graduated as class valedictorian. I excelled in everything that I did and every day I played a game to see whom I could beat. School was never work for me; it was something that came easily.

Once I had learned how to read, I began to absorb all the books I could get my hands on. I decided early that I wanted to write books—maybe even something as good as *Charlotte's Web*. I wasn't sure what I would write about and I didn't know if I had any talent. But, I knew that someday I would write books.

However, I figured that if I could not learn how to write, I would settle for being a social worker or an account executive at an advertising agency. There were three things I wanted when I grew up—to be an important person, to be needed, and to have influence in other people's lives.

I wanted to be important like my dad. I knew that people respected and liked him. My mom, also, was a woman of integrity and highly regarded in my community. I watched people who spoke with my parents and I knew that they believed in them.

I hoped, also, that I would be needed and strong like my mom and dad. I did not believe that they could do anything wrong. They made things work and they were never shaken by the small things that bothered me. I only wished that I could be so steady. But I knew that no matter what happened, they would always be there. So I tried not to worry about what would happen to me when I grew up.

For many years, as a result of bad business investments, my parents had money problems. I was blind to the problems until I was in fourth grade. I wanted to join the school band and asked my father to buy me a clarinet. And when he hesitated, trying to explain how hard money was to come by, I was shocked. I believed that he made thousands of dollars and I could not understand how one clarinet could kill him financially. He eventually agreed to buy me the instrument, but he constantly reminded me how much money it cost.

Some time after that, my brother was in an accident that cost my parents thousands of dollars. While walking home from a party one evening he was struck by a drunken driver who left the scene of the accident. It was hours before he was found, lying on the side of the road.

He was rushed to the nearest hospital, bleeding with internal injuries. He also had a broken leg, external cuts, and a fractured skull. Specialists were helicoptered in from Norfolk, Virginia, to try to save his life. My father, who was out of town on a business trip, rushed home just in time to see him come out of surgery. We all stood outside his door while the doctors pronounced doom.

I shall never forget looking at him for what I thought would be the last time—his head and body bandaged, an oxygen tent covering him. For the first time in my life I was struck with stark-naked fear. Knowing there was nothing I could do for him, I was overcome by tears of utter hopelessness. I wanted to wake him up and reassure him that I loved him. I knew that I had to beg forgiveness for all the times I'd gotten him in trouble. I felt that I had to beg him to live. And I started to cry, "Please don't let him die, don't let him go away."

Several days passed before he came out of the coma. He was able to mumble a few words, but the pain was evident in his eyes. He needed no words to tell me what he felt. And as he slowly began to recover he developed a brain hemorrhage and was rushed, by ambulance, to a larger hospital. I watched the doctors lift him into the ambulance and as they pushed him back I started to scream at him, "Don't you go and die on me, I'll never forgive you."

It was many months before my brother could even begin to live a normal life again. But his bandaged body reminded me daily of the fragility of life—that life is not forever and that at any time it can be taken away from us. I learned the value of telling people what we think of them before they are gone.

But the added bills of doctors, specialists, and hospitals were more than my parents could handle. Pressure was at its peak and they grew desperate. The amount of liquor they drank increased. Before that time, drinking had been a social pleasure, and a martini was something they had after work, before dinner, and maybe after. They always drank more than I was comfortable with, but now they began to drink in excess.

And the drinking increased any marital problems they had been having. Before this time, I knew that things were not always o.k. But, it was different now. Things were never o.k.

I noticed that my father did not make a point of being home after work. Often, he did not come home until after I was asleep. I knew that he was out at a bar, and when I was able to forget, my mother would remind me. Taking my sister and me by the arm, she would insist that we get into the car and go with her to look for him. If she found him, we had to sit in the car until she was done yelling at him. Then we'd drive home, my mother shouting and cursing all the way.

As she'd wait for him to drive in the driveway, my mother would pour herself a drink, and then another and another. If he was out an hour or more, she would be completely drunk by the time he got home. Then the battle would begin.

The fights would often last all night, and I was unable to sleep through them. It was like standing between two boxers. Every blow they threw landed in my face. I had to listen to the anger, the curses, the bitterness and arguments over money and drinking.

My mother's life slowly began to deteriorate. It was not uncommon to come home and find her lying drunk, passed out on the couch. Her bottles of vodka were hidden in her closet and my sister and I would find them and pour the liquor down the drain. For each we took, a new one appeared.

Sometimes, she would sit for hours and cry. I did not understand why she was so upset, for my parents never talked openly or civilly about their problems. Everything was kept under cover until a blowup occurred. Then all hell would break loose, as hatred, anger, and bitterness flew back and forth between them. My mother would scream that she wanted a family, that she needed my father home at night to help her. And he would yell back that he was trying to provide her with the money to make a decent home. Neither gave in.

The hardest thing for me was not that my father didn't come home. What hurt so badly was to see my mother lying on the couch, drunk, spewing out her anger and bitterness. Sometimes she would call me into the living room and put her head on my shoulder and just cry. Tears soaked my clothes and I tried to tell her that it would be o.k. But she didn't believe me. No matter what I did to comfort her, nothing helped. She just wanted to die and I didn't know how to answer.

My parents' pain became my own. My heart and my loyalty were divided. My mother would tell me her side of the story and I would think she was right. And then my father would tell me his— and I didn't know whom to believe. I began to hate both of them and the way they carried on. There was no room left in their lives for me and I was pushed into a very lonely corner. The childhood security was gone. I could not rely on my mother for anything, because I never knew when she would be drunk or sober. I could not turn to my father because he was never home. The house was a battleground that I wanted no part of, and I began to find ways to be away as much as possible.

I started to hang out with a crowd of people who were old enough to drive cars and buy beer. Many of them were friends of my sisters or brother. At first I was very insecure in this new group of friends and the best way to win their confidence was to out-drink them.

I pitched in for beer and vodka and kept up with their drinking. It was the only way to be accepted in the group. Over a period of time I developed a tolerance and could drink more than anyone I knew. I began to be known for this in my town.

In keeping up with this group of people, I felt that I had to be "tough." I would insist that I didn't really need anyone and was fully capable of making it on my own. My reputation spread into a neighboring town and a group of girls decided to test my toughness. They probably hoped that they could give me a real scare, but when challenged to a fight by their leader, I readily accepted. I was not ready to give up my title.

The group of us walked out to a parking lot. Donna, the leader, threw a punch my way. I ducked and leaped at her and grabbed her from behind. With my arm around her neck, I tripped her, threw her to the ground and jumped on top of her. Her face was to the ground and I began to rub it in the dirt. Two of her friends, standing by, ignored her pleas for help, and when I was finished with her I stood up and swore to kill the next person who tried to lay a hand on me. But I was scared to death that anyone else would challenge me. I didn't like fighting and didn't want to hurt anyone. I just wanted to be able to exist, but I was building a reputation that would be hard to live down.

Almost everyone I knew went to the drag-car races twenty miles away. And some of my friends, including my brother, drove on Saturday nights. When I was twelve I started to go, with much hesitation on my mother's part. But when I assured her that I would be good and get home early, she gave in. It was here that I met Bobby. He was a man in his middle twenties who was married and had two kids. He knew of me through my sister Anne and my brother. And one night he offered me a ride home.

I was intrigued by his interest in me, so I accepted, hoping my mother wouldn't find out; I hoped she would be drunk that night when I got home. I was grateful for her drinking problem when I found her asleep on the couch.

But that night began a relationship that took me many years to break. It was rumored in town that it was sexual, which was the furthest thing from the truth. I had found a friend who I could rely on and talk to. Often he would come around at two or three in the morning and I would climb out my window to meet him. We'd ride around town and eventually park at some beach. Then we would talk. I could tell him about the things that were going on at home and how much I hated it and he would listen and promise me that someday it would be all right. I believed in him and I trusted the things he said to me. He seemed to know so many things and had a confidence in himself that I had never seen in anyone. I admired his strength.

My parents, I believe, were always aware of this association. But the only one who ever tried to stop it was Anne. She threatened to expose me completely if I didn't quit seeing him. Little did she realize that that was what I really wanted. I wished that someone would notice that I was still alive. I was testing my parents to the limit, and not a word was said. When I realized that they weren't going to punish me, I stopped seeing Bobby.

I continued hanging around with a fast crowd and started to drink in the morning before I went to school. Often I was noticeably drunk when I arrived. But teachers, counselors, and the principal said nothing. Everyone ignored it.

Some of my friends' parents got wind of the things I was doing and my best friend was not allowed to come into my house—and I was banned from hers. Town gossips carried the stories of my life to the limit and spread scandalous material that was worse than *True Story*. I don't know where they got their material, but they made Redd Foxx look like a kid. By the time the stories got back to me they were totally blown out of proportion. "Why me?" I thought. The things I was doing were not uncommon in my town, although I was probably the youngest participant.

My grades in school that year fell drastically. I was now making high C's and low B's where once I had had no problem in pulling straight A's. Because of the late-night fights, I was tired when I arrived in school. My mind was preoccupied with family problems, and I could not concentrate on school work. I stopped studying and lost interest in everything they were teaching.

I began to disrupt class and instigate pranks on other kids. My self-image reached an all-time low, and I wanted to hurt people before they hurt me. I was afraid of total rejection from my peers.

An overwhelming sense of not being wanted or needed controlled my life. Sometimes I felt that I did not really exist and I would lie in bed wondering if I was real. "Who are you?" I would ask myself. And I could not come up with an answer.

There was a terrible feeling of loneliness and desertion that I could not dispel. Friends did not make me feel better. I was beginning to feel cheap because of the things I was doing. I believed that the older kids kept me around only because I was entertaining when I was drunk. I had become, in my own eyes, a cheap thrill.

But, my mother continued to tell me that someday I would make her very proud. I couldn't understand how she could believe that my life would ever be productive. Everything inside me told me that I was bad.

I tried to talk with teachers at school. At one point I saw a school psychologist. The best they could offer me was to say that in five years I'd be out and on my own. I knew that I could never survive another five years. I couldn't look anyone in the eye. When I walked down Main Street and saw someone coming, I would cross the street so I wouldn't have to look them in the face or speak to them. I was sure that they would hurt me by saying something cruel. I knew that it would make me cry and I didn't want anyone to see me with tears in my eyes. I was too strong to cry. The anger and bitterness knotted in my chest.

What hurt most was that no one offered help. Friends, close friends, stood by and watched me become more and more unhappy and proportionately more wild. My parents never asked me what was wrong. No one except the local gossips seemed to notice all the things I was doing. There was no encouragement to do better in school. My reward for low grades was five dollars each reporting period, and I knew I didn't deserve it.

Life was really cheap. Shame and guilt consumed me. Every promise I made to myself to try to do better failed. Life became gray—I watched a slow death. But no one said a word. Everyone I knew—teachers, friends, neighbors—stood by and watched; I was either condemned or ignored. I knew that sooner or later something—or someone—had to give. I had the feeling that it would be me.

One Saturday night I was pushed past my point of tolerance. I had been out with friends and when I walked in the door, my mother stood glaring at me. I knew by one look at her eyes that I was in for trouble.

Having lost all the respect I once had for her, I walked past her toward my room without saying a word. She was drunk and started screaming at me about the late hours I was keeping, the friends I kept company with, and the very apparent disorder in my life. I knew that I did not deserve the verbal abuse she was throwing my way. She ran past me and blocked the bedroom door so I couldn't enter. I asked her to move so I could go to bed. But she kept shouting, insisting that I answer her.

I lifted my hand and punched her in the face. And as she fell to the floor, I stood there screaming, "I hate you, I hate you!!" My brother, hearing all the noise and seeing my mother on the floor walked up to me and slapped me in the face. I ducked into my room and slammed the door. Now, both of them stood outside screaming obscenities at me and demanding that I come out.

I dropped on my bed and pulled my pillow over my head, tears soaking my sheets. "What have I done wrong? Why do they hate me? How will I get out of here?" I thought. As I crawled into a little ball and shook violently with fear and anger, my head began to spin and I felt that I was moving in circles through the air. I couldn't stop myself and I panicked because I had lost control. I could not stop crying, my stomach hurt, and I felt as though I was going to throw up.

I waited until I knew that everyone had gone to bed. My father had not come home yet. And when the lights went out and the house was quiet for a while, I carefully opened my door and peeked into the hall. It was safe. I tiptoed to the bathroom and opened the medicine cabinet. I picked up the first prescription bottle that I saw was full. Then I filled the bathroom glass with water.

Just as carefully, I tiptoed back to my room. Opening the bottle, I stuffed all the pills into my mouth and washed them down with water. Then I crawled into bed and closed my eyes.

3 Fathers, Provoke Not Your Children

I awoke the next morning, my whole body in cramps. As I tried to stand and walk to the bathroom, the room spun, hurling me to the floor. I could not stand without holding onto something, I couldn't hold my head up straight and was having a difficult time breathing. I inched my way to the window and threw it open. My head hanging out, I vomited and continued until cramps gripped my insides as I dry heaved.

The pills had taken their toll and most of the medicine was already in my system. I knew that I belonged in a hospital but I was so frightened by what I had done that I dared not tell anyone. It would become something else for my parents to argue about. And my mother would have another reason to drink.

I crawled back into my bed and reached for the bottle the pills had been in. I had taken my mother's thyroid medicine. Lying in bed, I wondered if I was going to die. I drew my legs up close to my body and pulled a blanket over my head. If I was going to die I wanted to be alone. Alone, far, far away from my mother. No noise, no yelling, no fights, no arguments, no booze. Alone!

I spent the whole day in bed, drifting in and out of consciousness. Two or three times I heard a knock and a voice. "I'm sick," I mumbled and rolled over again. "Leave me alone!" I didn't want to see anyone and I couldn't get up to answer the door.

The day passed and then the night. Sun streaming in my window woke me up the next morning. I opened my eyes. I was still alive. I could walk again and hold my head straight. Weakly, I opened my door and walked to the bathroom. Fear struck me as I brushed my teeth. Did my father know? Would my mother punish me for hitting her? Would she notice that her pills were gone? I stumbled back into my room and threw the bottle out the window into the woods. I was safe.

A note from my mother awaited me on the kitchen door: CALL ME. I picked up the phone and dialed her work number, cringing as she said hello. "Are you feeling better?"

"Yeah, I'm o.k. When you gonna be home?"

"Around six. Will you start the roast?"

"Sure, see you later."

I was home free. Either she didn't remember or she had chosen to forget that I hit her. My father didn't know and she wouldn't punish me. It was o.k.

But nothing had changed. As time moved on, my mother took up permanent residence on the living-room couch. Her magazines, cigarettes, and drink sat on the coffee table. Her pillow and blankets draped one corner. I would try to avoid the room as much as possible and often entered the house through the back door. But more and more frequently she would call me into the living room.

Drink in hand, tears streaming down her face, she'd throw her head on my shoulder and pour her heart out. "He doesn't love us. I don't want to die but I'm gonna die. I'm gonna die! Help me, Judy, make it better. Please make it better."

"I'll make it better, Mom," I'd say and I'd pick her head up off my shoulder and run into my room in tears. "Why doesn't he love her? why doesn't he love any of us?" Then I picked up a large cocoanut he had brought me back from one of his business trips and I threw it against the wall. "I hate him," I screamed, and ran out of the house.

I tried to talk to my father about my mother when he was home. "Don't hate her," he'd say. "She's sick."

"So why don't you do anything about it?" I'd answer.

"I don't know what to do."

"Put her away somewhere where she can get help," I whispered.

"No, she'll get better."

But she didn't. When she was extremely upset and had been drinking a lot, she'd call to me. And, sheepishly, I'd walk to the living room, wondering what she'd say. And one night as I walked into the room, she yelled, "Judy, we're leaving."

Before I had a chance to answer, she grabbed me by the arm and started pulling me out the door. "Where are we going?" I asked.

"I don't know, we're just going."

We climbed in the car and she started the ignition. Turning on the lights, she started to cry. She dropped her head on the steering wheel and began to beg me never to leave her. And then she passed out.

I didn't know what to do, so I tried to wake her up. When she came to she asked me where we were. I told her we were in the front yard. I turned off the lights and cut the ignition. "He doesn't love us," she mumbled. She mumbled things I couldn't understand because she was so drunk, and then she passed out again. I stayed with her the whole night, and when she woke up in the morning she didn't remember what had happened. I had to get ready for school and left her sitting at the wheel.

I hated my father for not being home during times like that. When he wasn't home, she leaned on me and I wasn't strong enough to hold her up. I was having a difficult time just keeping myself together. I had not only the burden of my own problems, I carried the burden of hers. I began to believe that my father didn't really love me. He was never there to protect me from her. And if he could cop out of the responsibility of caring for her, why couldn't I?

I decided that I could, but my mother, within all her turmoil, must have sensed this and it was not too long afterward that my parents told me that my mother was going away.

They made plans for her to admit herself to a hospital for observation and rest. After she had had a chance to talk out her problems and find solutions she planned on coming home and starting over again. My father offered to do anything he could to help her, but this was the only thing she would agree to do.

One summer day my uncle arrived to drive my mother to the hospital. The days before had been tense as she had almost lost contact with reality. She would sit for hours in a chair in the living room, her face to the corner, crying and saying things that no one could understand. When you tried to get near her she would yell and scream—wanting everyone to stay far away from her. She didn't eat and didn't move at night. She just sat, drink in hand, staring at the corner of the room. It was extremely frightening to see her reduced to such hopelessness. But on the day my uncle arrived, she snapped out of it and was ready to go.

My Aunt Myrna came by to help her pack and see her off. The house was quiet and no one said a word about her leaving. We were all afraid of saying something that would set her off. I, wanting nothing to do whatsoever with the whole affair, stayed in my room reading a book and listening to the radio. I was happy yet sad to see her leave. Was there something I could have done to make it easier for her? Part of it, I believed, had to be my fault and a wave of guilt engulfed me. I didn't love her enough and I hadn't tried to help her as I could have.

I had failed.

I heard everyone in the living room making their good-byes. But I dared not venture out. Then I heard my door open and as I looked up my mother was standing over me. My guilt and hate nearly overwhelmed me as I looked her in the eyes. I didn't want to kiss her good-bye. As she leaned over me and put her arms around me I was tempted to push her back and tell her to get out of my room. I wanted to scream and kick and fight, but I had no fight left in me. So, I let her kiss me good-bye.

"She should die and never come back," I thought. And then I wished that I had never thought it. I *knew* that she was never coming back. Deep down inside me I *knew*.

The house, after she had gone, was so empty. The fighting and the screaming stopped. They were replaced by a dead silence that nothing could fill. I couldn't feel her presence anymore, and it was as if she had never been with us at all. I wondered sometimes if she had really died, not simply gone away.

Death penetrated the house. When I came home from school there was no one there to ask me how my day had been. Nothing was planned for dinner. And it seemed as if nothing further had been planned for life. Life had ended for me, yet all around me, life went on as usual. I couldn't understand why the world just didn't stop. I wanted it to stop so someone could explain to me what had happened. How could things so easily turn so bad?

My father tried to explain to me that things like this happen. Some nights he would come home and I would make him a martini and broil him a steak. We'd sit at the kitchen table, facing each other, with little to say. I would take bites of his steak as he told me how his day had gone. But the conversation eventually turned to my mother. One evening he broke down and cried. I had never seen tears in his eyes and had no idea that way down underneath he loved her so much.

After she had been in the hospital for a few weeks, my mother decided to come home and try to make things work. But, the day she walked in the house she had a six-pack of beer in her hand. I stood, in shock, as she opened the door. Knowing that nothing had changed, I waited for the ax to fall, and within two weeks it was evident to all of us that she had not found solutions to any of her problems. It was with many tears that she left again—this time complete with U-Haul carting all her things. She was gone for good.

Often she would call us or my father would make us call her. And on Easter vacation I would take a bus to her new home. She lived in a tiny apartment in a very small town and had found a job that barely paid her expenses. The strain of seeing her made it impossible for me to stay long, and after only a few days I wanted to go home. I had nothing to say to her and was so edgy that all I did was argue the whole time I was there. After a few trips of this kind I begged my father never to make me go back and see her again. I hated her.

Seeing her life deteriorate made me blame my father for her leaving and for all her problems. Enraged by what I felt he had done to her, I put up a wall between us that would keep us as far away from each other as possible. I avoided sitting and talking with him. Staying away from home as often as I could, I made myself scarce.

And he, in his own loneliness, was not home often either. He was often out of town for business.

It appeared that he really did not care because he did not make it a point to be home when it really mattered—dinnertime, weekends, and when I needed him. What my mother had said—he really does not love us—began to penetrate deep within my heart. And my heart iced over.

I turned to my friends. I had entered high school that fall, and most of my lifelong friends were in a different homeroom than I was. Feeling lost, I began to turn to another older crowd where I could feel safe and secure. I desperately needed someone to lean on and someone to tell me that I was o.k. And these people accepted me with no questions asked.

The problem, however, was that this group of kids was experimenting with sex. Before this time I had not thought about it too seriously. I knew that I would wait until I was married, for that was the way it was supposed to be. I really had no interest in messing around, especially since one of my girl friends got pregnant that year. She was only fifteen.

But the pressure was always there. Sex was *the* topic of conversations and I often felt very out of place. The girls made it sound so interesting and normal, but I had no intention of doing the things they did. Their lives were cheap.

But in hanging around with them, I was always exposed to the things they did. And over a period of a year, it began to wear me down. I started to think there was nothing wrong with it. The philosophy went something like this: you can do anything you want as long as you don't get caught. That included sex, drinking, staying out late—or all night—and cutting school. This was the way my friends lived their lives.

And I began to do the same. I obtained false identification that said I was eighteen. Since I looked older than I was, I had no trouble getting into the local bars. My father was often away or out late at night so I took that as license to stay out late or not come home at all. I could always say that I had tried to call earlier in the evening and not gotten an answer. And I knew, of course, that he would not mind my staying at a girl friend's house. I was learning all the tricks.

One evening while out with my crowd of friends, I ran into a friend of Bobby's—an older man who I had known for a few years. I had not seen him in quite some time and sat down to talk. He started to buy me beers and succeeded in getting me very drunk. At that point, he asked me if he could drive me home. Intrigued by his interest in me, I said yes.

On the way home, he pulled off on a side road and drove into the woods. I was extremely drunk and really didn't notice where he was going. When he stopped the car, he put his arm around me and started to kiss me. Not really knowing how to react, my mind working too slowly to think about what was happening, I gave in to his advances and we had sex in the back seat of his car. A year of peer pressure, a lot of booze, and a compromising situation had taken its toll.

Looking in the mirror the next morning, I was relieved that I didn't look any different. I was sure that I'd be a dead giveaway. Immediately, I called my best girl friend Ann and told her what had happened. Instead of telling me how wrong it was, she welcomed me to the adult world and told me that I had finally done the right thing. Now I really belonged.

So, when Steve called me and asked me to go out again, I said yes. Convinced that I belonged to him forever and ever, I continued to see him week after week. I was sure that he would take care of me and treat me right. Eventually, he offered me money— forty dollars a night—and not knowing what that meant, I took the money and started to buy myself clothes.

I didn't tell anyone, because the money was my secret and I didn't know how other people would react to it.

Ann, seeing how readily I had taken to this life, put me up for even a greater dare. She knew a group of guys from another town who were very wild and had a reputation for getting into a lot of trouble. She challenged me to go out with them—she, of course, coming along—to go drinking and sleep with one of the guys. I, having entered the "anything goes" crowd, could not think of a reason to say no. I saw it as a test I had to pass in order to maintain her friendship.

But there was always a part of me telling me that what I was doing was wrong. I always drowned that part in a six-pack of beer before I could go through with it. And each time it became easier and easier to close my eyes and squelch the screams of protest within myself. If I were to say that I would not go out one evening, I was threatened by physical violence and scandalous rumors. What amazes me to this day is that none of my close, lifelong friends ever found out what I was doing and I was able to maintain a good reputation within my old circle. But, my double life was pretty hard to keep up.

I desperately craved acceptance. I did not care on what terms I was accepted, just so long as I knew that I belonged somewhere. This led to my throwing large beer parties at my house when my father was out of town. When I was providing someone with a good time, I felt needed.

My father unknowingly interrupted this partying life when he began to bring a few dates home to meet us kids. Since he had company, I had to be good and make a respectable presentation. So I would put on my best manners. I knew that I would be in for big trouble if I acted up. He continued, after a while, to date one woman named Joan. It seemed serious from the start and her occasional presence was threatening. The first time I met her I did not like her. She was too neat and too sophisticated for me. She lived in a city where people were more polished. And I hated the city people who poured into my home town every summer. I knew that if anyone could shatter my world of sex, older men, and drinking, this woman could. She looked at me as though she knew what I was thinking and I didn't like it. I felt as though I had been caught.

That autumn, amid my father's period of romance, my sister Phyllis married a man who was stationed on an army base in Texas. My brother had recently entered the Navy, and now I was the only one left with my father. Things were not looking good, because the house had been put up for sale. I had been asked to start cleaning out all the rooms and I knew that it would not be long before we would have to move. My father was not looking for a new place to live, and my suspicions were affirmed when I learned one day that he intended to marry Joan within a month of his divorce from my mother. My heart fell to my stomach as he told me that we would move to her house. First my mother had left, then my brother. My sister followed close behind and now the house would be gone. I fell into a deep depression.

All I wanted to do was stay in my room. Getting up in the morning and forcing myself to go to school was a chore. I had no desire to see my friends or go out at night. Crying was the only thing that felt good, as it brought release from the things I felt inside. I could not sort out all the thoughts in my mind. Was I cracking up?

The junior class at my school was putting on *Our Town* and getting a part in the play snapped me out of it. There were rehearsals almost every night, and I was too busy to think about the things that echoed through my head.

When she was in town, Joan tried to talk to me. But I wanted to stay far, far away from her. The melancholy mood I had drifted into persuaded my father to send me to Maryland to visit an old friend for a week.

I arrived, hoping that she would be someone I could talk to. But instead of being sympathetic, she also started to get on my case. My skirts were too short, my hair wasn't right, I hung out with the wrong people, and on and on. Nothing about me made her happy. She did not have a good word to say to me the whole time I was there. I left for home, deciding that I would never see her again. And I set my mind on accepting the fact that I would have to leave my home and go somewhere new.

The wedding approached very quickly, and took place on December 16, 1969. Joan had asked me to be in the wedding party, but to this day I do not remember the wedding or the reception. I blocked it out of my mind.

As they left for their honeymoon, I continued to clean out the house and pack the last of my things. I was the only one home, and the house was an empty shell of its former days. I would sit on my bed, looking out the window at the neighborhood around me. The sight was familiar and I knew every part of the landscape. I had grown up looking out that window and seeing the same sights every day. I would see them no more. My life was over here. This was the end.

I didn't understand, after so many years, how people could just up and leave their home. I had lost everything and no one could comprehend the blackness that enveloped me. Without thinking, I walked to the bathroom and took a new razor out of the medicine cabinet. It was thin and bent to the side as I started to slice my wrists—the left and then the right. Each cut was made a little deeper until blood started to spurt all over me. "Come on, bleed faster," I shouted and started to slice again, "bleed so I can die."

As the blood trickled down my arms I climbed into bed and pulled the sheet up over me. "This is the way it should be," I thought. "This is the way it should end. Nobody has the right to take so much away from any person!"

I awoke the next morning, my wrists swollen with pain. The sheet was covered with blood that had dried stiff in the night. Not knowing what to do, I picked up the phone and called my girl friend Sandi. She demanded that I get in my car and drive immediately to her house. I dressed carefully, so as not to open the oozing wounds on my wrist. Then I headed downstairs and climbed in my Chevy.

Shifting gears was a painful ordeal. My whole arm ached and I was sure that I could not take the pain. I made my way to Sandi's house in first gear and snuck into the house and up to her room. She took one look at me and started to cry. "Oh, Judy, I am so sorry this happened. I am so sorry for you."

Tears filled my eyes and I threw my arms around her neck. "Sandi, I hate it. I hate what's happening to me. Please don't let me go."

"Come on," she said, "let's get these things fixed up." As she walked me to the bathroom she put her arm around me and told me that it would be o.k. And like a little child, I sat as she, like a mother, bandaged my wounds. And we cried like two schoolgirls who had lost our loves.

My father and new stepmother, upon arriving home and seeing my bandaged wrists, did not say a word. They knew what had happened, and one day, out of the blue, Joan suggested that I see a social worker who was a friend of hers. We had moved into her house only the day before and she picked up the phone and made an appointment for me.

Cary was a kind and gentle woman who was just a little bit too friendly with Joan for me to be comfortable with her. Once a week she would take me to the ice rink and we would skate in circles talking to each other.

She asked me about my mother and father and what the family had been like. I found her questions difficult to answer as I felt she would go back and tell Joan anything I said. So, I made small talk for the months I saw her and finally she moved away or went to Europe.

School in this new town was frightening and lonely. The population was four times what it had been in my school. The kids were more sophisticated and congregated in groups that seemed ominous. I didn't even know how to begin making friends. I had never had to make friends, because all my life I had grown up with the same kids. I was now the outsider. I was not sure if I had what it takes to start over. Every insecurity in my life surfaced until I was paralyzed with fear and suspicion. I no longer trusted anyone. Cutting classes, I would sit in the girls' room and cry. When I had a study hall I would sneak into the Guidance Office and talk with my counselor, Mr. Henry. And on days when I felt totally incapable of facing this new life, I would not attend school at all.

But the confusion inside me made me feel that it was impossible to work out my problems. I would sit up late at night, writing letters to friends, short stories, and poems. Barricaded within my room, I often refused to come out at all. At least within those four walls I did not have to deal with the many issues in my life. There was no stepmother to face, no father to argue with, and no pain.

Often my father would come to the door and demand that I come out and join the family. I would walk to the door and lock it, saying that I was doing homework or writing a letter. Nicely he would ask me again to come out. When I said no, an argument would start and he would pound on the door, ordering me to come out. This made me more obstinate as I deliberately disobeyed his request.

Joan, believing that someone had to have control over me, would join in the fight. "It's time you learned who's the adult and who's the child in this house. Do what your father tells you."

"Go to hell," I'd scream, "and leave me alone."

Joan became edgy around me and would often accuse me of doing things I had no intention of doing. "You're trying to break up our marriage," she said. "And I won't let you get away with it."

"It's all in your head," I'd answer, and walk out and slam the door.

No matter what I did, she believed that I had evil intentions and completely distrusted me. In return, I came to hate her and wanted nothing to do with her. Finally, when the cat escaped from the house one day and she accused me of intentionally letting him out, I decided to just ignore her and remained coolly detached from the family.

That spring my father decided to let me go "home" on weekends to visit my friends. Each Friday I would pack a bag and head home. When I drove out of their driveway, there was a sense of release from the tension. The good times that I had with my friends helped me to temporarily forget my problems. It was not until I headed back on Sunday afternoon that the dark cloud of hate surrounded me like fog.

I would begin to steam with hostility and bitterness when I entered the driveway. "She" was the cause of my having to leave my home town. She was the one who had taken what little was left of my life. And she wanted me to adjust neatly and nicely to her way of life so that I could make her happy—and not disturb her serenity. "Fat chance," I thought. "She made her bed, now let her lie in it."

But, more than hating her, I hated myself. I felt ugly and unloved. No one could see things from my point of view, yet I was constantly asked to view the situation as they did. I was asked to be what I could not be—happy and cheerful—as if I didn't mind at all what they had done to my life. "Accept it," they said. If only it was that easy.

As spring arrived, my father and Joan made plans to move back "home" for the summer. Since one of his offices was located there, he thought it would be the perfect place to rest and try to pull the family together. I looked forward to going home and was able, one weekend before we moved, to secure a position in the produce department of a local Shopwell.

After moving, I felt that I was home free. Being among my friends at night and at work during the day took my mind off the family. I made it a point to be home as little as possible, and a girl friend picked me up every night after work to go out. I was home only to shower and sleep and rarely made it for dinner.

My dad became disturbed that I had cut the family completely out of my life. A few times he called me to his office and lectured me on being a part of the family. "Joan tries," he said, "to make you a part of her life. She wants you to be happy, but you don't make it easy."

"I don't like her," I answered, "and I don't care what she does. I don't want to be near her."

"I know it's not easy, but try."

"Yes," I answered, "I'll try."

But I didn't. I couldn't have cared less what she wanted or thought. She was an intruder and deserved what she was getting. If she had left all of us alone a long time ago, we would be better off. She would be happy, I would be happy, my father would be happy, and everything would be fine.

My dad sensed my inflexibility, and finally one afternoon he and Joan sat me down. "You really don't want to live with us, do you?" she asked.

"No, I don't want any part of you," I mumbled, my head to the floor.

"Well, we have decided that if you don't like it here you should go live with your mother."

"Fine," I answered, "I'll call her tonight."

I really did not want to go to my mother's, but in retaliation I felt that I had to. Being called on the carpet was a challenge to me and I knew that I could show them how tough I was. Picking up the phone, I swallowed my pride and dialed my mother's number. I explained the situation to her, and she agreed to come pick me up a few days before school started. I began to pack.

I spent the night before we left at my Aunt Myrna's, as did my mother. Early in the morning, we loaded the car and headed to her town. The drive was long and tedious and I wondered how I had ever gotten myself into this mess. I didn't want to live with my mother. I hated her more than I hated Joan. But, there was nowhere to go. I'd have to stick it out for one more year and then I could go to college and get away from all of them.

I registered at the local high school as a senior. One look at the place and I knew that I wasn't staying long. It was small, ugly, and oppressive. The first days of school I came home and announced that I wanted to go back to my father's. Enraged, my mother screamed at me as I called him on the phone.

"Can I come home?" I asked.

"Have you had enough?" he questioned.

"Yeah."

"Well, you can come home, but it's gonna be a lot different. Take a bus and I'll talk to you when you get here."

I rode home, hoping that everyone would be waiting for me with open arms. But to my surprise there was no brass band playing my tune. Both my father and Joan looked very stern as he said, "You cannot stay with us. We can't have the family disrupted this way."

"Oh, God," I thought. "They're gonna send me to reform school."

4 He Is a Friend to the Fatherless

I stood staring coolly at my father and Joan. "He has some nerve," I thought. "This is probably one of the few times he has ever gotten involved in my life—but only because it makes his life uncomfortable. I'm supposed to forget all the times he wasn't there, all the times I needed him and he wasn't around—or he was too busy. After all this, I am the bad guy. I get all the blame. And he wants to get rid of me. Nothing has changed."

"Do whatever you want to do with me," I said, "I don't care anymore."

"Well, you ought to care, young lady," said Joan. "It's your life and we don't know what to do with you. We don't know what you want from life. Obviously, you don't want to be with us. But it's time you started making your own life and decided what you want to do. We can't do that for you."

"We've decided to let you go live with Aunt Myrna," he said. "I've talked with her and she said you could finish your senior year at her house. You will be able to go back to your old school. What you do after that is up to you. I have no money to send you to college. Business has been very bad this year and I can hardly meet my bills. I have no money for you."

"Good old Aunt Myrna," I thought. "She's always there in a crisis." And so she had been all my life. As long as I could remember, she had tried to make me know that she loved me—no matter what happened. Even before I knew that family problems were bad, she was right there, spending time with me and telling me that she loved me.

When I was a child, she was the only relative I was close to or really loved. Often I would go with Phyllis and spend a whole weekend at her house. My cousin Audrey was only a year and a half younger than I and she was there to play with. But often, when Audrey and Phyllis went out to swing on the swing, I would sit in the house with Aunt Myrna and help her cook and clean. Sometimes I would sit at her feet on a little stool and just talk to her. As a young child, I knew that I was special to her, if not anyone else. She was my good buddy.

Uncle Ed I was never sure about. He was a quiet, standoffish man whom I never felt close to. I was more afraid of him than anything else. For many years, before they built their own home, they lived in a very old house that was dark and musty. I saw Uncle Ed as being very much like that old house. He wasn't someone I wanted to know well.

But Aunt Myrna was full of life and understanding. After my mother left, on weekends when my father was away, she would stop over or at least call to see how we were doing. Usually we were up to no good, and she had a way of calling or dropping in during one of our beer parties. But she never had a critical word. She just had a way of letting you know that she was thinking of you and cared about your life.

"Well," I said to my father and Joan. "It's better this way, I suppose. It's better for everyone."

Moving into and getting used to Aunt Myrna's was an easy business. When she had built her house, she had put in an extra bedroom "hoping that one day one of you girls would come stay with me."

"Funny," I thought, "that she should know how things would end up." I wondered where she got her inside information.

Home life was very different than what I was used to. Here, I felt respected and trusted. I no longer had the need to be tough or defensive. There was so little to protect because I was given privacy and space to be myself.

With Audrey there, I had a friend to talk to and get close to.

We had never become close buddies, and Audrey had believed all these years that Aunt Myrna loved me more than her. Many times during that year it proved true. I was not one much for being a favorite, and didn't like anyone to make a fuss over me. Audrey accepted this, with an occasional grunt and groan, and we managed to become like sisters.

Knowing that I had been on my own for so long Aunt Myrna did not strap me down with strict rules and discipline. This made it easy for me and made me feel very comfortable. I didn't want to hurt her, so I made myself go out of my way to be good.

The pressure of all the years behind me was gone. But being away from home for six months had drastically changed me. I was no longer interested in getting into trouble. All of that had been wiped out of me. I had no interest in guys and did not want to get involved deeply with anyone. I just wanted to be left alone to figure out who I was and what I wanted.

During my senior year, I began to think about my future and the course that I wanted my life to take. The years of "fooling around" had taught me that trouble and heartbreak were not foods on which one could build a life. I had no desire to live that kind of life any longer and in my new seriousness I realized that I was growing up and had to plan a future for myself.

This was the time in life when I considered my next move. I had only two choices. Either I could go to college and get a degree or I could work in the local Shopwell as a cashier. I could not see spending my whole life in my home town, never getting away to find out what the world was like. So, I decided that I must go to college.

Many of my friends were applying to state and private colleges and universities. I had no idea where I wanted to go. One day, upon walking into the Guidance Office, I closed my eyes and pointed at a map that showed the state universities. Whatever state university was closest to where I pointed my finger was where I'd go. After three attempts, I had decided upon three— one of which had to accept me.

My grades, however, had slipped during the previous three years. I was no longer in the top 5 per cent of my class, as I had been all through elementary and junior high. And I knew that in order to get into college, I had to make a big comeback in the following six months. I had to *prove* that I was able and willing to study and work hard. Methodically, I set my mind on a 90 per cent for that year and began to work.

In the meantime, I started to send out my applications to the colleges "of my choice." Even though state universities were cheaper than private colleges, I knew that I would need at least two thousand dollars each year to pull me through. Also, I would need spending money—something which I did not have. The reality of the costs and problems hit me like a ton of bricks.

I remembered my father's words: "I have no money for you." His business had more recently gone bankrupt and I could not depend on him for anything. So I set my mind on finding a way to finance my education.

I talked with my good buddy George one day about my problems. He had been brought up Catholic and believed in the power of prayer. I didn't know if he ever prayed, but he suggested that I begin to ask God to provide the money for me. I stood looking at him for a moment, thinking that idea was a little absurd. And then I said, "Why not?"

I began, that evening, my personal campaign to find God and any money He might have. I had been raised in the Baptist Church and had been told every Sunday that Jesus loved me. And now I had the perfect opportunity to find out if that was so. Nothing like a crisis to get you on your knees.

Wherever I had gone, I had moved my Bible along with me. It was now sitting on my shelf, covered with dust. I picked it up, not knowing where to start reading. I found myself in the Gospels, reading the words of Jesus. "The way is hard and the road is narrow. . . ." As those words rang through my mind, I started to cry. It had been hard for me the past few years. Maybe God was telling me that he understood.

Every night before I went to bed, I would take out my Bible, read for an hour or more, and then pray. I had many things to say to God because I had never talked with Him before. My mind was full of "whys"—concerning the pattern my life had taken. There was so much that I just didn't understand. But, as I prayed and poured my heart out before Him, a sense of peace came over me, that I had never felt before. I began to know that Jesus loved me—although He seemed so far away.

In complete boldness, I asked God to provide the eight thousand dollars I needed to complete my college education. I believed that nothing was impossible for Him—after all, He was God. I had no idea how He was going to get the money to me, but I trusted that He would. There was not a doubt in my mind.

One day, upon arriving at school, there was a message for me to see my guidance counselor. I rushed to his office. He sat me down to tell me about a new program for kids like me. "The program," he said, "is specifically for blacks. But they will take people who are educationally, financially, and culturally deprived."

I looked at him for a moment and then answered, "I don't care who it's for, let's just get me into it."

"O.k.," he said, as he pulled out the long forms he had been sent. We filled them out, I all the while realizing this was my only chance to get a college education.

"Don't fail me now, God," I whispered, as he sealed the envelope. "Don't fail me now."

I would often sit and think about what I wanted to study at school. Up to this point, I had thought that one day I would just "know" what I was going to do for the rest of my life and from there on in it would be easy. But nothing like that happened to me. I remembered saying that I wanted to be a social worker. But it seemed so far away. I wrestled with the idea of being an account executive at an advertising agency. "How do you get that kind of job?" I asked myself. "I can always become a famous writer," I thought. But, then I had to laugh at myself. Only famous people wrote books. And who was I? "Well, if worse comes to worst, I'll be a teacher," I decided. It seemed the easiest way out.

Making these plans and deciding on my future brought yet another change into my life. I discovered that I was no longer a child, but a woman. I had always taken care to dress neatly and comb my hair nicely. I'd always worn just enough makeup to highlight my strong features. I had been conscious of my sexuality, but never of my womanhood.

How special and wonderful I felt. Being a tomboy for so many years had left little room for my femininity. Aunt Myrna had been pushing me, for years, to wear white frilly blouses and all those feminine things. But, I had not had any interest in them. I was happy to wear an old pair of jeans and an old shirt.

But, this year things were different. I suddenly liked to dress up a little, adding a touch of jewelry and changing my hair color. I wanted to identify with the "new me" that was emerging. The craziness of the past was gone. I wanted to leave behind the cheapness of my early teens and become beautiful. I didn't want to be used anymore. The time that I was spending on Scripture was having an influence in my life—although I did not know what it was at the time. I developed a new sense of dignity that I'd never had and I didn't want to lose it.

I dropped all my old crazy friends. I dropped my second life. And I began to spend time with the girls I'd known all my life. I became involved in their "girlish" talks and escapades, feeling that this was a big part of being a woman. I had been given a new life. And I was ready to leave the old one behind.

I often went out on weekends with my girl friend Mona, and Carl. Mona had been my best friend for ten years, although we often drifted apart during that time. She was safe company. Her boy friend, Carl, thought that I was a very funny person, and often asked her to ask me along on their dates. The three of us became a team.

One evening when we were out, Carl was talking to a guy I'd never seen before. We were all sitting at a table, drinking beer, and this new guy, Mike, leaned over to make conversation with me. I had nothing to say to him, since men were presently out of my league. I didn't want to get involved with anyone and most of all didn't want to encourage anyone to get involved with me.

I snubbed him as best I could, and turned my head to talk with people who were on my left.

The next day Mona called to tell me that Mike wanted to go out with me. "I don't know," I said. "I am not really interested in seeing anyone right now. You know what I've been through. And you know how I feel about guys. I don't think I can handle it, Mona."

"We'll go with you, Judy," she answered. "Carl and I will pick

you up and we'll all go to his place for dinner. He has food there
that you and I can cook and it'll really be o.k."

"I don't know, Mona," I said. "I don't trust men. How do I
know what he wants from me?"

"Don't worry, I'll be there and you don't have to do anything
you don't want to do."

"O.k.," I said reluctantly. "But you'd better not leave me."

That Friday, I dressed with care but was extremely tense about .
going out with this stranger. I hadn't dated anyone in a long time,
and I wasn't even going out with guys I knew. I'd never seen this
guy in town before. And I knew *everyone*. "He must have just
moved here," I thought. But Carl acted as though he'd known
him for a long time. "Something is not right," I thought. But I
ran to the door when Mona and Carl honked the horn.

We arrived at his house—one of the old, beautiful houses on
the top of a mountain outside of town. The wooded area was
most private and *very* rich. After walking through the door, I was
put at ease. Mike gave us all a tour of the house—which was filled
with treasures from all around the world. "My father's things," he
said, as we passed from room to room. I was noticeably impressed,
but returned with Mona to cook dinner in the kitchen.

Dinner conversation was hard, but drinking a few vodka col-
linses made it easier. Mike talked little about himself and tried to
pull me out of my shell. He was kind and gentle—something that
I liked very much. But I still didn't trust him.

The next morning, Mona told me that Carl had told her that
Mike was a friend of Bobby's—the married man I had seen when
I was thirteen. "Oh no," I thought, "here we go again. What am
I getting into?" My mind started to click as I realized that he
must have heard of my past escapades and was just trying to use
me for what he could get.

That evening he called me. "I don't know who you are or what
you want from me," I said. "But I know that you're a friend of
Bobby's and you probably know too much about me. Well, that's
all behind me and I don't want any part of that kind of thing
again. Leave me alone." And I hung up.

The phone didn't ring for three days. And then Mike tried
again.

"Look," I said, "I told you how I feel. I don't want to be used by you or anyone else, for that matter. I've made a new life for myself and you aren't going to ruin it."

"Listen," he said, "I don't know what you are talking about. I haven't seen Bobby in years. I had no idea that you went out with him, but I certainly don't want to use you or hurt you. I'd just like to get to know you better."

"Leave me alone," I said. And I hung up.

A week later the phone rang again. "Please see me," he said. "I really don't want to hurt you." I hung up.

Two days later the phone rang again. "Please see me this Friday."

"O.k.," I said, "but you'd better not try anything." "This man is going to have to win my trust," I thought.

Although I saw him regularly, he knew that I didn't trust him. Mike didn't push me and didn't try to get anything out of me. He really enjoyed my company. This amused me to no end, and I started to enjoy being with him. Over a matter of months, we became good friends and the inevitable happened; I fell hopelessly in love with him.

The most difficult aspect of the relationship was that he'd be out of town for days and often for a week at a time. I asked him where he went and what he did, but he evaded my questions and promised to bring me back cartons of cigarettes. And while he was away, he would call to tell me that he loved me and was thinking of me. I began to think that I had found the man I would marry. I thought that perhaps I should put off college and find out if this relationship was really serious.

When Mike was "in town," I spent all my time with him. He had an extra car that he didn't use and he gave it to me. It was an old, run-down Ford that needed a lot of work. But it got me where I was going.

I soon realized, however, that there was much about Mike's life that he wouldn't tell me. I knew that he was hiding things from me, but I couldn't imagine what they were. Often, when I was at his place, the phone would ring. And he'd go into another room and talk to the person on the other end for what seemed like hours. When I asked him who it was, he wouldn't tell me.

He also drank too much. It seemed as if he was drinking all the time now—morning, afternoon, and evening. Often, when he was blasted, he would start to tell me stories about people who had died. And he would cry as he described, in detail, what people do when you shoot them in the stomach or the head. I, not understanding any of this, wondered if he was going nuts. There was so much about his life that I found to be a large mystery. Why this big house? Why did he have so much money—sometimes a thousand dollars or more in his wallet? Why was he gone for so many days during the week? And where did he go?

As I questioned him, over and over again, he became so defensive that I decided it was best to drop the subject. "You sound like a wife," he said, "or my mother. Leave me alone." Mike was on edge constantly and often sat watching the phone and waiting for it to ring.

One day, while he was out shopping, the phone rang. He had told me never to answer it, but I thought that maybe it was him. I picked it up. "Did you place a long distance call to South Africa?" someone asked. "No, I didn't," I answered. "Is this 569-8335?" she asked again. "Yes, it is," I answered. "Your call is ready to go through." "Look," I said, "You must have the wrong number." And I hung up.

Mike came home and I told him about the call. He flew into a rage. "I told you never to answer the phone, they won't like it," he said.

"Who are *they*?" I yelled back. "Who are *they*? You always talk about *them*, but you won't tell me who *they* are," I screamed.

"The *Family*," he yelled. "Do you know who 'The Family' is?"

"Sure," I said, "tell me another one." I walked out of the house and drove home.

I didn't call Mike for a while and waited for things to cool off. When I finally called him, he said that he couldn't see me anymore. "*They* don't want you around," he said.

"Sure," I said, "you're the one who doesn't want me around. You don't have to lie to me. I get the message."

A week later Mike called to make up. "Look, baby," he said, "I'm sorry. Things just aren't going right for me lately and I'm uptight. I didn't mean to scream at you."

"It's all right," I said, "I understand." But over and over again I kept thinking, "He needs psychiatric help."

I began to see him again at his place on weekends. He never seemed to want to go out of the house. So, week after week, we sat, listening to the radio or watching TV. Not at all my idea of a good time.

One evening in particular, he fell asleep as we were watching a late-night program. I let him doze off, thinking that I would wake him later when I was ready to leave. As I was concentrating on the TV program, I heard the back door bell ring. "Who can *that* be?" I thought, as I got up to answer.

There was a man standing outside and I was unsure about letting him in. "Open up, I want to see Mike," he said. "A friend," I thought, my mind a little hazy from the late hour. As I opened the door a crack, the man pushed it open and put a .45 revolver to my head. My eyes almost popped out of their sockets, but I held back my scream. "This is just another part of the nightmare," I thought. "I'd better be cool."

With the .45 to my temple, he walked me to the living room where Mike was sleeping. He shook Mike, pointing to the gun at my head. "Van," Mike said, "put the gun down. She's o.k."

Van dropped the gun to his side and I gave a big sigh of relief. "I'd better get home," I said, as I rushed to the back door.

Mike followed close behind, giving me a look of understanding as he opened it. "See you soon, baby," he said.

"Not if I can help it," I thought.

I hopped in his car, starting the engine as fast as I could. I left tire marks as I headed down the road. "Oh, God," I thought. "He really is into something. How did I get into this mess? What am I going to do? Who can I tell?" I swerved around the corner at the bottom of the hill and tried to relax as I drove home, calculating my next move.

Trying to regain my composure, I noticed that a car was following me. I was still shaking from having a gun pointed at my head and I watched the car make every turn I made. I couldn't see who was driving it, but it was a newer-model Chevy. "This is it," I thought. "They're really after me." I stepped on the gas a little to see if the car would fall behind. It didn't. And when I finally entered my driveway, it slowed down almost to a stop while I pulled into the garage.

The following week, I tried to put everything out of my mind. I didn't want to believe all of what my mind told me because it seemed too preposterous and way out to be real. "These things don't happen in small towns," I convinced myself. "There is a good explanation." I didn't dare call Mike. I just *didn't* want to know what was going on.

A week later Mike called me. "Meet me at the tavern at eight o'clock," he said, "and don't let anyone see you walk in there."

"You make it sound so easy," I said. "*What is going on?*"

"I'll tell you when you get there."

I hopped in his car and made my way to the tavern. His car was in the parking lot, so I snuck in the back door. Mike was waiting for me at a table in the corner.

"Judy, I want you to know what is going on. I can't tell you much. They don't like you because they think you know too much. And they want me to get rid of you."

"Hey," I said, "I don't even know what you're into."

"My job, baby," he answered, "is to 'get rid' of people who don't follow company orders."

"Sure," I said, "and my name is Cinderella. Let's talk about something else."

"We have to talk about this. I can't be seen with you anymore. They are watching you." The scene of being followed home flashed through my mind. "If you're good and don't say a word, they won't bother you. But, if you start talking, I'm the one who will have to do you in."

"Why did you get me into this? Why didn't you just let me alone? I told you from the start that I wanted nothing to do with you. I didn't want any trouble. But, you just pulled me right into this. Nice friend you are, real nice friend!"

"Baby," he said, "I needed someone, too. I needed someone to talk to. Judy, I love you, do you believe that? I really love you. But it's just not going to work out."

I sat and stared at him. "Why," I asked myself, "do I have such a way of finding trouble? Even if I don't look for it, it finds its way to me."

"Judy, let's just cool it for a while. When I can see you, I'll call you. Things are a little rough right now."

"Sure," I said, as I ordered a beer. "Life is rough. I know."

I rode home that evening wondering if all he had told me was true. I remembered the phone call, the days he was away. And I remembered Van. But I didn't want to believe it. I was in a fairy tale that would end soon and everything would be back the way it used to be. Defiantly, I drove to his house the next day and walked right in.

Van was sitting in a lounge chair, swinging his gun around his finger. Mike just stood and looked at me with shock written all over his face. "I told you not to come here!"

"Oh, leave her alone, Mike," Van said. "Hey, little kid, you want a job? If you really want a part of the action, I can get you in. There's *no way out*, you know, but it pays well. I'll give you two hundred and fifty dollars a week to relay messages to our people across the state."

"You're all crazy," I said. "And I don't believe a word of what you tell me. You're not even Italian."

"You're right, little kid," Van said. "But we get the job done. Don't we, Mike?"

"Mike, I want to talk to you alone," I said. "Come here." He followed me to the bedroom and sat down next to me. "I don't care what kind of trouble you're in. I know you can get yourself out of it. But I love you. I want to marry you."

"It can't be that way, baby," he said. "You go to college like a good little girl and I'll work this out my way. You can't be involved."

"Mike, I don't believe what you tell me. I just can't believe it."

"It's o.k.," he said. "You don't have to. I'm the one who *has* to believe it. You've been accepted at that school, you know?" he said.

"I have?" I answered.

"Yeah, I found out today. Only problem is that you are on the first floor of the dorm. It's too easy for them to get you there. One day some men will drive up in a black car and knock on your door. They'll say I sent for you. But, if you get in that car with them, you're never coming back. I know what they'll do. So, I'm working on having you moved to a different dorm on a higher floor. It's harder to get to you there."

"I don't believe you," I said. "You're going crazy and you should have your head examined."

"Yeah, I probably should."

I left with the agreement that Mike would call me when it was safe.

"I can't see you because we're 'taking care' of some guys who messed up. When it's over, I'll call you."

"Safe?" I thought as I was riding home. "*Safe,* who's *safe?*" I watched the traffic drive past me. "It's more like *sane.* Call me when you're *sane,*" I mumbled under my breath.

Within a week I received a notice that I had been accepted at Willis State College. And I had also been accepted into their special program for "disadvantaged" persons.

I was stunned. My prayers had been answered. I was home free. I ran down to the local Baptist church and sat, saying my thank-you's. "Oh, God," I said. "You really are alive. You really do care. I don't know what to say." Tears spilled from my eyes, as I felt for the first time in my life that someone was on "my team," pulling for me, seeing things from my point of view.

My rooming assignment arrived within a few days. Just as Mike had said, I was to be living on the first floor of a dorm. I stared at the notice in shock. Two weeks later I received another letter. My rooming assignment had been changed. I was moved to the third floor of a dorm located next to the administration building.

At least a part of his story, then, must have been true. I wasn't sure which part. But I was so confused. I couldn't believe he could hurt anyone. He was a kind and gentle man. Putting a gun to someone's head and blowing them away seemed totally out of Mike's league.

"Not Mike," I argued with myself. "Not Mike."

I got a job at Henderson Park that summer as a lifeguard. Some evenings Mike would call me and ask me to come over after work. I felt like a human yo-yo, never understanding his signals.

"I'm going away to New York," he said, "and I'll be gone for at least a year. The heat's on and I have to hide for a while. It's good-bye, baby."

He made good-bye look so easy. There was no pain on his face, no sorrow, no regrets. Just like that, he was going to leave. No tears, no strain.

I put my arms around him and sobbed. "I love you, Mike, no matter what you do or who you are. I really love you."

"Do one thing for yourself when you get to school," he said. "Keep your mouth shut. I'll be watching you."

I looked into his eyes and read his face. He was seriously threatening me. I stepped back and swallowed hard.

"You would really hurt me if you had to, wouldn't you?" I asked.

"If I *had* to," he answered. And I walked out the door knowing that I had not seen the last of him or his friends.

5   Teach a Child in the Way He Should Go

Entering college that fall, I slipped into what appeared to be a world of total freedom. Freedom from restraint, freedom from rules, society, parents, and laws. I was now an adult—whether I was ready or not—and I had to make my own choices. There was no one standing behind me saying, "Do this, do that." I'd been waiting for this all my life.

"Now," I thought, "I will be able to find out who I am." There were new people to meet, new experiences to try out, and many choices ahead of me which offered me a whole new life. Isn't that what I had wanted?

Maybe so. But never had I felt so vulnerable. The decisions I would be making would have a bearing on me for the rest of my life. Living in a community whose values were "relative," was not much different from the "anything goes" crowd I had fled when I was seventeen.

The first thing I noticed when I arrived on campus was that almost everyone was a "freak." The student movement of the sixties was coming to an end, but the life style and philosophy of "freakdom" was still in full swing. "Thou shalt hassle the establishment and rebel against society" was the first bylaw of the "in" group.

I tried to take in this new atmosphere and somehow make sense of it. But it was full of contradictions that I couldn't reconcile. The community was full of people who were failures and would never go anywhere. For the first time in my life, I saw junkies who always looked as if they were on the verge of death. I saw people living in old, filthy apartments, with little desire to rise above their circumstances. What bothered me most were the rich kids who went out and spent hundreds of dollars to "look like a freak." That was the ultimate contradiction of the philosophy—the campus madness. But, everyone was trying to find out who they were. Sometimes I felt like I was just a player in a game that had been rigged. I didn't see that there was anywhere to go. Everyone checkmated everyone else. And there was always someone ready to knock down what you believed was truth. Everyone was confused.

I spent my first two weeks at college trying to sort all this out and see where I fit into the scheme of things. Totally overwhelmed by it all, I thought that perhaps I should just live my life and not think about the rest of humanity . . . but then I met Dick.

I met him at a local tavern called the Boat House. I was out with my next-door neighbor, June, when Dick walked right up to me and started talking. I was no better at handling men than I had been five years before and was extremely unsure of myself. I wasn't about to let Dick get to first base with me.

"Where are you from?" he asked.

"Alaska," I answered.

"Oh, it must be cold up there."

"Yeah, it is, but I come from a long line of tough Eskimos who don't let it get to them."

"Wow," he said, "I never met an Eskimo before."

"Yeah," I thought to myself, "and you probably never will."

For many weeks, I let Dick believe I was an Eskimo. I knew that it was a lie, but if he was stupid enough to believe it, I wasn't going to destroy his illusion.

He turned out to be, however, a very good friend. He was faithful, loving, kind, and gentle—qualities which I readily admired. We spent many hours and evenings together. But he was so easily won over that I began to dislike him. "Why does he find me so lovable?" I'd ask myself. "Why doesn't he dislike anything about me?" I felt like a Madonna that had just been placed on a pedestal where it didn't belong.

Dick was so available. Whenever I needed him, I knew that I could call and he'd come running. If I wanted to go to McDonald's at midnight, he'd rush over in his car and drive me there.

"No one should love anyone that much," I thought, as I tested him week after week to see how far his love would go. I found no limit. "He's so dull," I thought. Too steady, too reliable, and very unexciting.

It was not long before he took me home to meet his parents. And they loved me, too. I could see the picture running through their minds—me, in a long white dress, flowers in hand. Him, in a tuxedo. That weekend as we walked through a mall, he stopped at a jewelry store window and pointed to rings. I knew that it was time to take flight. Although I needed his friendship and love, I didn't want to be trapped. I carefully planned my strategy for maintaining the friendship while killing the romance. But it didn't look easy.

There was, however, one thing I knew would make him angry. Drugs. I hadn't tried any kind of drug. I just had never seen any point to it. I was not on a cosmic-awareness trip, like many of my friends, but I couldn't see that there was any harm in using them now and then for pleasure or for trickery. This would be a perfect way of putting a wedge between Dick and me. It would ruin all his plans.

Joe, my next door neighbor's boy friend, knocked on my door one evening as I was studying for a math test. "Bored?" he asked me.

"Yeah," I said, "I just can't get into this tonight."

"Want to do something different?" he asked.

"Like what?" I questioned.

He put his hand in his pocket and pulled out two small orange tablets. I stared at them and looked up at Joe. "It's Orange Sunshine," he said, "good old LSD."

"Really?" I whispered, looking around to make sure no one saw us standing at the door. "I've never seen it before."

"Want to trip with me?" he asked.

I closed my eyes and swallowed hard. "Sure," I answered. "I've got nothing else to do."

We raced off to Joe's room like two little kids sneaking behind the barn to smoke a cigarette. As Joe took out a razor and cut the tablet in half, a sense of exhilaration went through my body. I swallowed my half convinced I'd just committed a cardinal sin.

Joe turned on the stereo and dimmed the lights. The black light he turned on lit up all the fluorescent paints he had dabbed on everything in his room. I looked around the room and noticed that he had pictures of the devil on three of his walls. As I slipped into my new world, I glanced up at them. They were laughing at me. I laughed back.

My trip was far from the mind-expanding experience I'd heard that other people had. There were beautiful colors and the walls and floors seemed to melt as I stared at them. But I spent most of my time thinking that I was an oyster. For nine hours I sat and acted as I thought an oyster would act. At one point though, I jumped up and tried to hold up the ceiling. "What are you doing?" Joe asked me. "I'm playing God," I answered, "and I didn't know it could be so much fun." Eventually the drug wore off and I fell asleep on the floor listening to hard rock and watching the sun come up over the horizon.

The next day, upon waking, I felt as if my whole life had been changed. As burned out as I was, I thought that maybe I had come across a way to find the "real me." "I'm locked up inside myself," I thought, "and all I need is a way out." I walked across campus thinking this when I noticed some graffiti spray painted on a wall. "God is acid—Acid is god." "It's probably true," I thought.

I purposed, after that evening, to make my way into the freak crowd. There was a crowd of kids on campus known as the Willis Perennials. These people, so the legend was told, had been in college for five years or more and would probably be there for the next five. "They're taking it slow," someone told me. "That way they don't have to go out in that materialistic world." But, as I watched them, I began to suspect that they were all failures—by anyone's standards. They did nothing but take drugs, sleep, drink, and just exist. They were the people who sold drugs and I knew that I had to find a way into the crowd.

I told Dick about my trip.

"You fool," he said, "do you know what you are doing to your mind?"

"Yes," I answered, "I do. And if you don't like it, you can stay out of my life." I figured this would discourage him from pursuing my love any longer. Instead, it caused him great concern and he pulled even closer to me.

I began to smoke pot regularly after that, but acid made grass feel like kid stuff. I craved acid more and more.

As I moved into the drug crowd, I noticed something else I hadn't seen before. Every girl had a guy whom she hung out with and stayed with. Also, the "one night stand" was a popular game at that time. Why wasn't I getting any offers? What was wrong with me? I looked at myself in the mirror and examined my face and body. "I'm just as good as any of the girls out there," I told myself. Finally I went to Joe and asked him what was wrong. "What is it?" I questioned.

"There's nothing wrong with you," he said. "It's just that the guys respect you. They can't sleep with a friend."

"So why can't I be more than a friend?"

"I don't know," he answered.

My sexuality really needed a boost. I thought of Dick. "I know he loves me," I thought. So I dressed up one night and carefully put on my makeup. "This ought to get him," I told myself. And just as proudly, I pranced over to his room to see if I could arouse his interest. I walked into his room, thinking I could pull the scene off.

Dick glanced at me in surprise and immediately nodded to a stranger in the room. "Meet my new roommate, Andy," he said. I did a double take. This guy looked just like Mac Davis. "Hi," I said, "my name is Judy."

"We're doing the River Road run tonight," Dick said. "Want to come?" I stared at him for a moment as I mulled over the possibilities in my mind. River Road is the Main Street of Willis. Up and down the road, from one end to the other, is a series of bars that are open most of the night. The object of the game was to stop at every bar along the way and have one beer. As the legend goes, no one makes it to the end.

"Is Andy coming?" I asked.

"Yup, it will be just the three of us," Dick answered.

"Well, count me in!" I chuckled.

The three of us ran out to River Road and stuck out our thumbs. A car soon came by and took us to the other end—the starting gate. Slowly, we made our way across town, progressively more smashed at each stop we made. "Look, gang, I can't make it much farther," Dick said as we reached the next to last stop. "Well, you go on home," I said. "I'm sure that Andy and I can make it the rest of the way alone."

Dick left for home and Andy and I sat, sipping our beers. I asked Andy about his background and he told me stories of things that had happened to him in Vietnam. As he talked, he cringed and hung his head. "Hey," I said, "forget it. I didn't know that it was so painful to talk about. Why don't you come back to my place and we'll order submarines and talk some more."

"Sure," he answered.

We walked back to campus and I signed Andy into my dorm. Stumbling into my room, Andy fell on my bed and passed out. "Oh boy," I thought, "this guy is a real live wire." I pulled the covers over him and crawled into my roommate's bed, hoping she wouldn't come home that night.

Andy continued to call me, especially when he had been drinking. And he'd ask if he could come stay with me for the night. "I just want to be with you," he'd say.

"Sure," I'd say. I was pleased to have an affair going—just like all the girls I knew. It made me feel needed and wanted.

Dick knew what was going on, but he didn't say a word. I thought that this, and the drugs I was taking, would surely put him off. Instead, he saw it as a challenge to draw closer and fight harder for my affections. The invitations to visit his parents kept coming, and I kept accepting them. I began to be convinced that nothing was going to stop this guy from loving me—and that he had decided to wait for me until I got all my fantasies out of my system. And I was so intrigued by his faithfulness that I couldn't let go of him.

June, who had come to know Dick, kept insisting that he was square. I couldn't help but agree with her and often, when we would take acid, we would secretly dedicate our trip to Dick, in a sort of vindictive way. "Here's to Dick," June said, "who doesn't know how to have any fun." We laughed and joked about it, but I knew deep inside that Dick had it a lot more together than either one of us.

Sometimes I wondered if I should just give up fighting his love. I had never met anyone who cared about me the way he did, and I didn't know if I'd find another in the years to come. The problem, however, was that I wanted someone to sweep me off my feet. I just couldn't make myself feel romantic about him. And to me, romance was love. I couldn't have one without the other.

June lived in Andor, a large city fifty miles away, where my life-long friend Ann went to school. For many weeks we had talked about hitchhiking to Andor and visiting her. Finally, I called Ann and asked her if she had room to put us up.

"Come on down," she said. "A friend of mine just got a shipment of acid and we can trip over the weekend."

"All right!" I answered. June and I rushed to pack and then ran to the road and put out our thumbs.

Ann was ecstatic to see me. What pleased her more was that I was now a part of the drug culture and she had someone to trip with. "I have seventeen hits of four-way acid," she said. "But I found out that it's beat stuff. You have to take three just to get off. But," she continued, "it's better than nothing."

The three of us swallowed the acid and ran outside to "play" in the park. We were walking around deciding what to do, when the acid hit me. I felt as though I'd been struck with lightning. The acid I'd taken was not beat. I had taken three tabs of good, heavy acid, and I knew that I wouldn't come down for days. I tried not to get upset about it and walked around convincing myself that I "would come down."

Ann, June, and I walked all over campus, stopping here and there to watch a tree melt or stare at the beautiful colors passing through the air above us. Eventually we became tired and decided to rest at the local McDonald's. We walked in carefully, hoping no one would notice that we were high. We sat down with a sense of relief that no one had even looked our way.

Ann went to get us Cokes, and June and I sat talking about what we'd do next. When Ann returned, a guy walked by and stopped to talk with her. "Sit down," she said, "these are my friends Judy and June." I said hello, and he turned all his attention toward me. "Want to go to my place and smoke some dope?" he asked. I looked at Ann to see if this guy was "all right" and she gave me a nod and a look, saying he was.

"Look," I said, "I'll meet you guys later, at the apartment or something."

"O.k.," Ann said, "take it easy."

Ralph and I walked to his place, only a few blocks away. All the houses on his street were old and run down, and the farther we walked, the worse the neighborhood became. This made me edgy; I didn't even know this man. I knew that I was headed for trouble. As we made our way into his house, I saw that the paint was coming off the ceilings, the floors were dirty, and the place was really a tenement.

He unlocked his door and stepped inside in front of me. I entered carefully and as he turned on the light, I saw that the place was filthy from the floor to the ceiling. Beer cans were strewn all over, and everywhere I looked there were pills. "Some friends she has," I thought. "And she let me get into this."

I sat down, planning in the back of my mind how I was going to get out. I was still very high on acid, but I sensed that this guy was not good company and that I was in danger. My mind whirled as I planned my escape. Ralph lit a joint and passed it to me. "Just what I need," I thought as I took a toke. Suddenly panic hit me and I made my way to the door. "I have to go," I said.

"What's the rush, baby?" he asked.

"I just want to go," I said.

Ralph took my arm and pulled me over to the bed. "Sit down," he yelled. "You don't have to go. You just got here." Then he started to take off his shirt. "Look," I said, "you have this all wrong. I do have to go." I ran to the door, unlocked it, and ran out into the night. I kept running and running until I was out of the neighborhood. Then I looked back. He wasn't following me.

I made my way back to Ann's apartment. She and June had just arrived. "Some friend you have," I said, anger rising within me. "What did you set me up for?" I screamed. Ann looked at me, puzzled, as I explained what had happened. "How long have you known him?" I asked.

"Well, I don't really know him," she said. "I was only introduced to him a week ago. I don't think he's such a good character."

"You're telling me," I said. A sense of disgust came over me. She hadn't changed at all. She was just as careless and irresponsible as she'd always been. I wished I would come down from my trip so I could go home.

But it was impossible for any of us to sleep. We listened to the stereo for a while. As the sun rose, we knew that sleep was not on the agenda. We put on our coats and headed back outside, hoping we could walk off the drugs. The only place open that early in the morning was McDonald's. We made our way in for the second time and I decided to forget the evening that had passed and to concentrate on maintaining my sanity.

I sat fidgeting with my coat. Ann went to buy Cokes for us all and June sat next to me, jabbering. When I looked up, I noticed a man dressed all in black walk in. I turned my head away.

"Judy! Judy Lee!" he said, as he walked over to me. I looked up and stared him in the face. He was an older man, probably in his fifties. As he began to talk, he took off his black gloves and slapped them in his hand.

"I have a message for you from 'a friend': You have five hours to get out of town."

"What are you talking about?" I asked. My head was spinning and fear nearly paralyzed me. "You know who I'm talking about," he said. "And he doesn't like what you're doing. Get out of town."

Ann walked back, just in time to hear the end of the conversation.

The man looked at her before he turned and walked away. "He must be talking about Mike," she said. "And it wouldn't surprise me. I saw Van the other day."

"You saw Van?" I yelled. "What is he doing in Andor?"

"He was asking for you," she answered.

"For *me?*" I said. "What do they want from me? I haven't done anything."

"I don't know," she answered, "but you'd better get out of town."

My mind snapped back to the summer before. I remembered Mike's words to me. "I'll be watching you." I started to cry.

"Look," Ann said, "you don't have time to get emotional about this. You have to get out of here."

"Sure," I said, "I'm loaded to the gills on acid, my mind is all screwed up, I'm tired, and now I have to get out of town."

Ann took my hand and June just sat there wondering what was going on. "Let's go," she said. We walked out of McDonald's, back to her room and then to the bus station.

June and I sat in the bus station as I started to tell her the story of the year before. "You sure know how to pick them," she said. "I sure do," I sighed, as we walked onto the bus. "I sure do."

I arrived back on campus, still high. Paranoia had begun to get the better of me, so I went to my room and locked the door. "I'm never going out again," I thought to myself. "Next time they'll have a car waiting for me." I lay in bed, trying to sleep. Finally, it came.

I awoke two days later, my mind still full of thoughts of the days before. I wondered who, among my friends, was watching me. I felt that I couldn't trust any of them. But, then I remembered Andy. There was no way in the world that he could have any part of this; I knew he was clean. I picked up the phone and called him.

"Dick, let me speak to Andy," I said.

"You can't," he answered.

"Well, why not?" I asked.

"He moved into the fraternity house this weekend. He's not here anymore."

"Oh, that's real great! Do you have the number?" No sooner had he given it to me than I hung up and started dialing.

"Let me speak to Andy," I said. I could hear the shuffle of people and noise in the background. Finally Andy picked up the phone.

"Hi," he said. "What are you up to?"

"Listen," I said, "I don't have time for small talk. Can I come stay with you for a while?"

"What's the matter?" he asked.

"Don't ask me," I answered. "Just say yes, o.k.?"

"Yes," he said.

"Great, I'll be over in an hour."

I packed a small bag and headed downtown to the fraternity house. Andy was waiting for me at the door. "Look," he said, "you can stay for a few days, but this place is wild. You might not like it. And I don't know how the guys will like you being here."

"I don't care," I answered. "I just need a few days to think."

I stayed in the fraternity house for three days, thinking about what had happened. It all seemed so freaky to me. Was my life still in danger? It seemed too impossible to be true. Finally I got my mind together and decided to brave the outside world. I made my thanks and good-byes to Andy and stepped timidly out the door.

The paranoia that loomed over me like a dark, black cloud put me on edge. I wanted an assurance that I was going to be all right, but there was no way of knowing. I started to watch everything that was happening around me, listening to other people's conversations. I was sure that at any moment a man would walk up to me and drag me off. In fear, I turned to doing drugs, day after day losing myself in another world. I only wanted to escape.

Joe was always happy to find me drugs and often he would do acid with me. I didn't trust him anymore, and often thought he was a part of the plot against me. But, wanting to stay around him to find out if he really was, I took up his offers to do acid and party.

Acid has a funny way of affecting the mind. Whatever is happening in reality becomes totally distorted and bent. Acid alters your thinking and your perspective and can make you do some pretty wild things. As I did more and more acid, my thinking patterns changed.

One time Joe found some Purple Haze—a type of acid that Jimi Hendrix used to sing about. I had never done that kind before, but was willing to try anything. We went to Joe's dorm and sat in the lounge watching TV while we waited for the drug to take effect.

As I started to get high, I thought about all the things that had happened in the past few weeks. I looked at Joe and became totally convinced that he was the person who was ratting on me to Mike. "He's better off dead," I said to myself. As Joe watched TV, I snuck into his room and picked up a large, heavy, metal candlestick. "I'll hit him over the head and throw him out the window," I thought. "And people will think he jumped." Walking back to the lounge, I made my plans. And it never occurred to me that I was actually going to KILL someone. All I knew was that I was protecting myself and he had to go. I walked up behind him and struck him over the head.

His head dropped and he momentarily went unconscious. As he started to come to, I realized that I really intended to kill him. I dropped the candlestick because suddenly I knew that I couldn't do it. I couldn't kill my friend. "What are you doing?" he yelled as he regained his senses. "Have you flipped?"

"I don't know what got into me," I said, tears running down my face.

"Sit in that chair and don't move," he said, as he ran to his room to wipe the blood from his head.

"What am I doing?" I thought as he left. "What is happening to me, am I going crazy?" I sat there, knowing that I was losing grip with reality. I didn't really want to kill anyone. I was just so scared and I couldn't tell anyone about it. There was no one who would believe me.

Joe came back and sat to talk with me. "Judy, you're acting pretty strange lately," he said. I looked at him.

"Joe, you wouldn't understand," I answered. "I'm sorry, I just flipped out."

"Well, take it easy," he said. "Just take it easy."

But taking it easy wasn't easy for me. I felt compelled to do more drugs and more and more. I was running away from my fear, from myself, and from the threat on my life. I just wanted to die. I did more acid so that I wouldn't have to think about it.

Joe had a new girl friend named Kathy. And one night they invited me over to her place. I was happy to have something to do so I ran right over. Joe took out a four-way hit of Orange Sunshine and I sat watching TV as I waited to "get off."

As the drug began to hit, I knew that I was on my last trip. My mind started to jump from one thought to another. The things I had been thinking about became distorted and as I looked at Kathy and Joe, they turned into Mickey and Minnie Mouse.

I tried to talk to them to tell them that I was flipping out, but not a word would come out of my mouth. I pictured myself in a large, empty egg shell, unable to get out. I reached for the phone to call Dick, but Joe slammed it down and told me that I couldn't talk to anyone. I ran to the bathroom, thinking there would be a razor there that I could slit my wrists with. Joe sensed my panic and sent Kathy after me to stop me.

I tried to explain to them that I had flipped and was never coming back to the real world. "You'll come down," Joe said. "Just take it easy," he said. "Relax!" But I couldn't relax. I was in a whirl, everything around me looked unfamiliar and I knew that I had to die. I walked to the door, planning on going up to the tenth floor and jumping out the window.

But Joe pulled me back. He plopped me down in front of the TV. "Watch this until you come down," he yelled. "And don't move!"

I sat and tried to watch the FBI, but the program was about a scuffle with the Mafia. The top of my head almost blew right off and I started to scream. Joe and Kathy came running and sat on both sides of me. "You're going to make it," they said. "You are going to make it." I closed my eyes, believing that I wouldn't.

After a few hours, the effects of the drug began to wear off. I began to have a grip on reality and relaxed a little. But I knew that this trip had done me in and I was frightened to find out what the damage to my mind had been. I was more scared of coming down and finding out than I was of staying high forever.

Within nine hours, I had crashed. Too exhausted from the ordeal to think about where my head was at, I walked back to my room and tried to sleep. I had pains in my stomach because the acid had been laced with strychnine. I doubled up in cramps. If I could only find rest.

Kathy called the next day and asked how I was. I didn't want to talk to anyone. I had fallen into a deep depression and couldn't control all the thoughts that were going through my mind. "Well, listen, Jude. We're going to Washington, D.C., for a march and we thought you might like to come to get your mind off things," she said.

"Really," I said, perking up a little. "I've never been to a demonstration before. I'll go," I answered.

Joe, Kathy, their friend Alex, and I headed for Washington, D.C., the following day. On the way down, Joe prepared us for what might happen.

"There'll probably be fifty thousand people there," he said. "And more than likely we'll get arrested. Every year they have this May Day March and try to close down the city and every year someone gets arrested. But if we stick together, we'll be o.k."

We arrived late Friday night and made our way to Potomac Park. Kids from all over the country were filtering in, and the park was like a circus ground. As we walked through, we saw groups putting up tents for the weekend, people selling drugs, and many just sacked out on the ground. We found a place under a tree and tried to go to sleep.

We awoke the next day to hear the noise of bands setting up for a concert. People were all around us, reminiscent of Woodstock. We packed our things and made our way into the clearing where the concert would be. Finding a spot of our own, we set our things down and waited for the music to start. Meanwhile, hordes of hippies sat down around us until we were in the center of a sea of humanity.

As the Beach Boys got up to sing, I decided to take a walk around the reflecting pool. I crossed the street and stared at my face in the water. An antiwar chant rang out in the background and I hummed along.

But, my mind was preoccupied. "Can you really change things?" I asked no one in particular. "Can you *really*?" No answer came. "Well, is this the way to live, is this life?" I asked again. No answer. I turned to my right and kept walking.

"What if I get arrested?" I asked. "What if I get beat up?" Who will bail me out? Who will even know that I'm in jail?" I looked back at the concert behind me. I listened to the music. And suddenly everything seemed so useless. Life, the demonstration, the people I knew. "It's worthless," I thought. "Completely worthless."

I made my way back to the concert, a little depressed and disgusted with myself and life. Music raged the whole night until finally, in the morning, the D.C. cops surrounded the park and told everyone to get out—with threat of arrest.

"Come on," Joe said. "Let's get out of here." We picked up our things and walked back to Alex's car. "Why don't we get a motel room and get some sleep before the demonstration tomorrow," Joe suggested.

"Great," I said, "I could use the sleep."

We drove to Maryland and found a room. We ate lunch and talked the afternoon away. I dozed off as they turned on the TV and dreamed of getting arrested.

Early the next morning we headed to Georgetown, where people from our state were supposed to be demonstrating. We stayed in the car, riding around and waiting for the action to start. People were slowly drifting in, but we realized that most everyone had gone home after the concert. "Real radicals," I moaned to myself in disgust.

The demonstration started to gain momentum as the riot squad was called in to stop the people marching down the streets. Tear gas started to fly, and cops were knocking kids down with their cars and motorcycles. After they had knocked them down, they'd jump out and start beating them over the head with clubs. "Let's get out of here," I yelled. "I don't want any part of this."

Alex started to head out, when Joe yelled for him to stop. He pulled over and Joe jumped out and started running down the street. "We'd better follow him," Kathy said. "He's bound to get into trouble." Alex turned the car off and we all ran after Joe.

As we ran, a can of tear gas fell in front of us and cops grabbed us. "You're under arrest," they said as they smashed Joe over the head with a billy club. And all four of us were loaded into a bus, along with many other kids who were in the immediate area.

They drove us to the D.C. jail courtyard—where they loaded us with about a thousand other people. Cheers went up as we entered. Busloads of people kept coming in, until they announced that they were taking us to the Coliseum. Little by little, we were loaded back into the buses and dropped at the Coliseum.

What a sight that was—seven thousand hippies in one place.

Some were singing. Some were high. One kid took all his clothes off and started dancing around the crowd.

During this time we weren't given a lawyer or given our rights. The Civil Liberties Union was fighting for us because we had been arrested illegally. Finally, a lawyer was let in and he announced that if we paid ten dollars bail we could go. Cheers of "hurray" went up and people started to form a line to buy their way out.

Each person was processed, complete with mug shot and finger-prints. Kathy, Joe, Alex, and I made our way through and finally signed out at the door. "Let's get home," I said. "I can't take this anymore." As we started to the corner, a CBS crew made their way to us and started asking questions.

"What's going on inside?" they asked. "Is anyone hurt?"

Joe stepped forward to talk into the camera. "Those pigs . . ."

I turned my back to the camera. "Oh, God," I thought, "is there life after death?"

6 When You Search for Me with All Your Heart . . .

The end of the school year brought great relief. I knew that I could go home, slip into the role that was expected of me by my family and friends, and live a completely new life. I packed my VW Bug and began the tedious drive through Memorial Day traffic, all the while planning my vacation.

My sister Phyllis was in town that summer. Her husband was in Vietnam on the front lines and she had taken an apartment to be near the family. Feeling very lonely, she had extended an invitation for me to come live with her. I was thrilled not to have to go to my parents' or aunt's house. And the idea of playing with a three-year-old niece seemed like a wholesome change.

I arrived home, trying to shake the traumas of the past year from my system. Being in familiar surroundings gave me a great sense of peace and security. I had, however, gained twenty pounds during the school year. I went on a crash diet that brought me back to a weight that made me happy. Then, it was easy to regain some sense of "self."

Having my new "look," I decided that it was time I became a liberated woman. I wasn't sure what liberated women did, but I began my campaign by buying a few low-cut dresses that had to be worn braless. "This," I thought, "will find me a man who will love and cherish me and stand beside me no matter what happens." I was pleased to be living in the seventies, when people could be whatever they wanted to be.

I knew that I needed to find a job right away so I could start saving money for the school year ahead. I had written my old boss while I was still in school and stopped in to see if I could have my job back. He was happy to see me and asked me when I could start. Everything was going so smoothly that I thought maybe the tide had turned and life was on my side.

Living with my sister was easy. We had always been good friends and now we had time to renew our friendship. It seemed strange to me that she was married and had a family of her own. I didn't remember her that way. But, family or not, she was the same old Phyllis she had always been—loving, calm, and easygoing. I often sat looking at her, wondering how she had managed to stay so sane. How could anyone be so "normal"? I felt cheated.

And so, I began what appeared to be a very happy summer vacation. I felt good and thought that I had left my winter problems behind me. Life was easy, struggle was minimal, and there was so little conflict to deal with. "I have overcome," I thought, "the worst that I will ever go through. And I'm free from it all."

One morning, however, my sister came running into my room. "Judy," she said, "this came for you in the mail this morning." I took the letter from her hand and looked at the postmark. It had been mailed in New York. "I don't know anyone in New York," I said to Phyllis. "And I don't recognize the handwriting."

"Well, who's it from?" she asked me. I sat up as I opened the letter.

"It's from Mike," I answered, dropping my head on the pillow.

"Who's Mike?" Phyllis asked.

"You wouldn't want to know," I said.

"Really, who *is* he?" she asked again.

"Sit down for a minute," I answered. "You won't believe what I have to tell you."

Phyllis made herself comfortable on the edge of my bed as I told the story of Mike. Her mouth dropped wide open even though she was trying very hard not to look shocked. "Wow," she said, "is he for real?"

"I don't know," I answered. "I don't know what the real story is and I doubt if I ever will."

"Well," she said, "I don't want him in my house. Don't bring him home."

I began to read. "Judy, I love you and I'll be home in 2 weeks. Please meet me at the railroad station. I'll call you the night before I am scheduled to arrive."

I folded the letter and put it back in the envelope. Holding the letter in my hand and thinking over his message sent my head reeling. The love I had felt for him before I'd gone to school returned. But, it was counteracted by my anger and rage over what had happened during the winter. "Maybe he's out of trouble and has gone straight," I said to Phyllis. "Maybe it's all behind us and we can get married." I turned my head, hiding my tears.

"Look," she said. "Don't worry about it till you see him. You do have two weeks."

"I'm so confused," I answered as I got out of bed and dressed. "Why won't he quit haunting me?"

The night before his arrival, Mike called from Maryland. "Baby, I'll be home tomorrow at 5 P.M. Will you pick me up?" he said.

"Yeah," I answered, "but we have a lot of things to talk about."

"I know," he said, "and we'll have plenty of time for that."

I dressed with care the next afternoon, trying to look as attractive as possible. When I stared in the mirror, I saw a completely different person than when we last had seen each other. My hair was longer and was bleached from the sun. My figure had filled out around the hips. I smiled at myself in the mirror. Adding my last touches of makeup, I ran downstairs and hopped in my car.

As the train pulled in, I tensed up and tears again came. But, as Mike walked off the train, I couldn't help but run to him and throw my arms around his neck. He gave me a bear hug and then pushed me back and looked at me.

"When I left," he said, "you were a little girl. You've grown up into a beautiful woman." I looked at him and smiled.

"Mike," I said, "I have to talk to you about the past year."

"Look," he answered, "can't we leave that behind us? I was in trouble and you were heading for bigger trouble. I had to protect you."

"But, Mike," I answered, "you scared me out of my wits. I waited for *them* to come and take me away."

"Baby," he said, "I wouldn't send anyone to hurt you. I wouldn't harm you."

"But you threatened me before you left. I took that seriously and didn't know if someone was going to come wipe me out," I said.

"Let's talk about it later," he said. "Right now I just want to get home, unpack, and relax."

"O.k.," I answered. "Let's go."

We hopped in my car, heading for his house. Along the way we stopped at a grocery store and bought food. I looked at Mike out of the corner of my eye as I drove down the street. He looked different—subdued and almost broken. I hoped that it was only fatigue that I saw in his face. I couldn't bear to think that everything had changed in the year we'd been apart.

Arriving at his house, I put away the groceries and started cooking as he showered and unpacked. I felt out of place in his house. I no longer belonged there or to him. "He's just a lot of trouble," I whispered to myself. "I must be crazy to want any more of this. I must be crazy." I was tempted to walk right out and leave everything behind, but I couldn't do it. I couldn't just walk out on him.

Mike walked into the kitchen and put his arms around me. "It's so good to be with you again," he said, as he kissed me on the cheek. "I really missed you."

"So, why didn't you write? You could have dropped me a note or called me. You *knew* where I was. You knew everything I was doing. You knew who I was hanging around with and you could have made some kind of contact."

"I couldn't blow my cover, baby," he insisted. "I *couldn't* call you. But, things are better now. The Family is off my back and I'm almost free from this business. Almost free."

"Really?" I asked. "You really mean that? You're getting out!!"

"Yes," he answered. "I'm almost free."

"Oh, thank God," I yelled as I threw a dish towel into the air and gave Mike a big hug. "It's over!!"

During dinner, we began to talk about the things that had happened in the past year. There was so much to say, as so much time had been lost . . . and the gap was so wide. The year had put a wall between us that would prove hard to break. I had really changed. I wanted different things from life than I had a year before. I wanted my independence, and the chance to find myself. My identity was very important to me. "I should not," I thought, "be wrapped up in him." But, I couldn't tell Mike about that. I couldn't explain the wall that had come between us. I tried to pretend that everything was the same. It was so much easier.

I rode home that evening feeling torn and yet happy. I was glad that I had a man around with whom I could share my life. I liked having someone there to love me and care for me. But, he seemed so far removed from where I was heading. Mike was not a well-educated man. He was, perhaps, a bit too old fashioned for me. He was not the kind who would let me have a career and life of my own. His possessiveness guarded his security and manhood. I knew that I had a decision to make.

At work, I talked to my girl friend Gloria about my problem. "I love him," I told her, "but I also love the idea of having a life of my own."

"Listen, Judy," Gloria answered, "you don't have to see him if you don't want to. You don't have to continue the relationship. You can do whatever you want to do."

"Yeah, I know," I answered. "But I want both things. I don't want to make a compromise."

"Well," she answered, "think it over. You have time."

As I contemplated the situation and tried to piece together the events of the past two years, I felt trapped by my confusion and my circumstances. I experienced severe pressure and the old dark cloud that had penetrated my life at school returned. And with that were acid flashbacks that struck me at the height of my work day.

The middle afternoon hours were the worst at work. It seemed as if everyone came in during that time. I rushed around, helping people in what I considered a swift and efficient manner. But then an acid flashback would hit. I saw clouds of colors floating through the air. My mind went numb and I became dizzy. Staring at the customers, I would temporarily lose touch with reality. People would talk to me but I couldn't hear them.

Gloria saw this happen one afternoon and came running over to me. "Jerry," she said to one of the guys in our department, "take over here for a minute. Judy isn't feeling well and I want to take her to the ladies' room." She grabbed me by the arm and pulled me over to the side.

"Are you all right?" she asked. "You look like you just saw a ghost." I stood and stared at her without flinching. "Judy! Are you o.k.?" she asked again. I jumped when I heard my name and came back to reality.

"What did you say?" I asked.

"Are you *all right*? You look awful. What's wrong?"

I told Gloria about all the drugs I had taken the year before. I was frightened that the effect would never wear off and I would be subjected to these attacks for the rest of my life. "It takes all that I have to keep myself together," I told her. "I feel like I'm losing the battle."

"A little rest will help you a lot. Why don't you go home?"

I told my boss that I was ill and drove in a daze to my sister's. When I walked into the house Phyllis took one look at me and told me to sit down. "You're white as a sheet," she said to me. "Can I get you anything?"

"No," I said. "I'll be o.k. if I lie down." I got up and walked to my room. I knew that I was on dangerous ground. Losing my ability to think and concentrate made me feel that I was also losing all of my self-control. "I'm at the mercy of those stupid drugs," I thought. "And there's nothing that I can do about it. Who can help me?" I remembered Dick. I wrote him a letter, and poured my tear ducts and my heart out.

"Dick," I wrote, "You'll probably think I'm crazy, but then, so do I. Things just don't seem right. I can't hold onto life the way I used to. My mind doesn't work right anymore. I try to think about good things, but nothing looks good to me these days. Everything has turned black. I don't think there's a way out of it this time. I've reached the end." I signed the letter, sealed it, and dropped it in the mailbox. For a week I waited, not very patiently, for my answer.

The following Friday my answer came. I tore open the envelope, expecting to find my hope in Dick's words. "Judy," he wrote, "You have had a bad year. Maybe you should just rest for a while and try to take it easy. I imagine you have a lot to think about, but you'll be o.k. Love, Dick."

I stared at this and grew hot with anger. "He's a lot of help," I thought. "I'm about to crack up and he tells me to take it easy. How can I rest? I have a job, a relationship to work out, and school to face in the fall. And I'm falling apart. He's no help at all."

I tried to muster all the self-control I had left and finish out the summer. The attacks came more frequently and frazzled me to the limit of my tolerance. I was jumpy, paranoid, always on edge. My attitude grew defensive as the edges of my life gradually unraveled. I wished there was someone who would understand what I was feeling. But I knew of no one whom I could talk to. I surrendered to "fate" and decided to work things out on my own.

I didn't tell Mike what was happening. I knew that he would think I was being silly and just laugh it off. He wouldn't understand. Becoming quiet and often withdrawn, I handled the relationship the best I knew how. "Summer will be over soon and I can leave," I assured myself. "Nothing is forever." Mike accepted my silence, often thinking that I was tired from a hard day's work.

One evening he called me and asked me to come over right away. "I have a surprise for you," he said. "Get here soon."

I rode to his house, wondering what he was up to. Mike had talked about buying me a new car, and I thought that perhaps he had gone out and done it. I knew I couldn't accept such a gift. I entered his driveway, wishing that I could go right back home. I wasn't prepared for a surprise.

"Let's eat first," Mike said as I walked in. "And we'll talk later."

"Fine," I answered. Making myself at home in his kitchen, I prepared dinner. Afterward, we sat on the couch and Mike turned on the radio. In between small talk, he made us drinks, until he finally settled down and got to the point.

"Judy," he said as he put his arm around me. "I want you to marry me."

I just stared at him and said, "What?"

"I want you to marry me," he repeated. "I can't live without you."

I took his arm off my shoulder and pulled away from him. After an eternity of silence I said, "I don't know, Mike. It's hard for me to say yes." The intensity of the look on his face scared me.

"You have to marry me," he insisted. "You're all that I have left. I have no one but you, so you *have* to marry me."

"I do not," I replied. "I don't know if I can. I want so much more from life. I don't want to be stuck in a house for the next fifty years. I want a life of my own."

"I'll give you anything you want," he answered. "If you want a new car—I'll buy you one. If you want a beautiful wardrobe, I'll get that for you, too. I'll buy you a house. I'll do anything for you."

"I don't want those things," I yelled. "I want my freedom."

"You can't have it," he said, as he put his hands around my neck. "You can't have it, you have to marry me. If I can't have you, no one can." He started to squeeze my throat and then pulled a pillow from the couch and started to put it over my face, pushing down. "I won't let go of you," he yelled. "I won't let go. You belong to me."

I tried to scream and push him away. I went into a panic. "I'm too young to die," I thought. "Stop it," I screamed. "You're going to kill me." My screams were muffled by the pillow. My breath was getting short and when I could not take another minute of struggle, he took the pillow from my face and looked at me, his eyes empty and frightened like those of a beaten child.

I sat up. "You're insane," I screamed. "You were going to kill me." I stood, my whole body shaking. "You were going to kill me," I shouted again. I grabbed my bag and headed for the door. Mike stood in the living room shouting, "I'm sorry, I'm sorry, please come back." I ran to my car and drove away.

"I can't go home," I thought to myself. Still shaking, I could barely hold onto the wheel. As I drove through the next town and then the next it seemed as if time were standing still. Before I realized it, I was thirty miles from home. Slowly, I came to my senses. I looked at myself in the mirror. I was still alive.

"Thank you, God," I said. "I'm still here." I turned the car around and headed home. "I'm not going to die," I kept telling myself as I drove into the darkness.

Phyllis was up when I walked into the house, and asked me how my evening had been. I didn't want her to know what had happened, so I told her that things were fine.

"What was his surprise?" she asked me.

"Oh, he just had a nice dinner waiting for me," I answered. "I don't think that I'll see him anymore," I said. "I think I'll leave early for school this year and stop to see some friends along the way."

The last weeks of vacation dragged, and I did my best to get through them so I could go back to school. Mike called several times, but I refused to answer or return his calls. I pushed what had happened to the back of my mind and tried to forget it. Secretly I wondered if he would come to get me. "Probably not," I decided. I hoped that he would disappear from the face of the earth, never again to be seen by me, or anyone else.

I tried to motivate myself to get up, go to work and come home in the evening. But I just didn't care what happened. The acid flashbacks came and went and I braced myself to get through the hard times. "It will get better when I get back to school," I thought. "I'll be far, far away from everything."

But, I could not help but remember the year before. I had had so much emptiness inside me. Would this year really be better? The joy of living, the zest of fighting for myself had been knocked out of me. "Is it too much to ask that I should have a normal, sane life?" I asked myself. "Aren't there any normal people who want to be my friend?" I looked at myself in the mirror. "I'm not a *bad* person," I thought. "I'm really not bad compared to what's running around on the streets."

There was so little to believe in. People always either let me down or wanted to possess me. My work at school was so boring. I was sick of the parties, sick of the freak culture, sick of always having to play a game. All I wanted was to be real and to have someone love me. Someone who would let me love him back.

I left a week early for school, stopping along the way to visit friends. "You seem different," one said to me. "You're a lot more settled."

"Yeah," I answered. "I'm just plain tired of fighting. I want something to believe in."

"Well, believe in yourself," he said.

"Sure," I said. "Sure."

I arrived at school tired and defeated. "Nothing is worth working for," I told Kathy, my roommate that year. "Everything slips through my fingers like sand. If I had something to believe in, I know I'd feel a lot better."

"Well," she said. "Maybe you'll find a guy this year. That would make you happy, wouldn't it?"

"Yeah," I answered, "it would. But it just doesn't seem like anyone *good* ever wants me. I'll never find a guy."

"Yes you will," she mumbled. "You will."

Dick came to see me after I had unpacked and settled in my new room. "Feeling any better?" he asked.

"Yeah, I guess so," I answered coolly. "I had a rough summer and I just want *to be left alone.*" Still angry from his helpless letter, I looked at him, hoping that he'd get the hint.

"You deserve something good," he said. "And maybe this year you'll find it."

With little desire to party or prance around with my friends, I settled into classes and tried to immerse myself completely in my schoolwork. I bought myself an ounce of pot and often sat in my room alone, reading my textbooks and smoking a joint or thinking about life and all the things that had gone wrong. "Life isn't supposed to be so morbid," I thought. "There's got to be happiness somewhere." Deciding that it was something I hadn't earned the right to, I walled myself in my room, studied, smoked pot, and thought. I wanted to figure everything out before the next semester, so I could start it on the right foot.

Kathy didn't think that I was doing myself any favors by being alone so much. "You've got to get out of this room," she insisted.

"I can't be bothered," I answered.

"Well, there's someone I want you to meet, so I'll bring him here if you won't go out," she said.

"Great," I answered. "Bring on the troops."

The next day, Kathy brought home Ed. I stood up as he entered the room and said "Hi." "Hmm," I thought—"medium height, blond hair, blue eyes—the right combination for love." He had about him a beautiful aura of peace and acceptance. Life didn't unruffle him the way it did me. I liked his strength.

"I just broke up with my girl friend," he told me the first time we talked. "So, I'm trying to throw myself back into life."

"I can understand that," I answered.

"It's not easy," he said. "But you can't stop living." I smiled as I realized I'd found *the* one.

Ed spent a lot of time with me. "You're so comfortable to be with," he explained on one of our walks through the woods. "It makes it very easy to get to know you. There aren't many people in the world who can put people at ease, and maybe that's why I like you so much."

"Well," I answered. "You're not so bad yourself."

We grew very close and shared our intimate feelings with each other. Some evenings we would climb up on the campus hill and watch the sunset over the horizon. Other times he would call and ask me if I wanted to take a ride through the old country roads and then go out for dinner. "That's a great idea," I said. "I just love to drive." I'd grab for my coat, and run downstairs to wait for him at the door.

The friendship reached the point where it had to become romantic or it had to be cooled. Since I had already decided which I wanted, the decision was up to Ed, and sure enough, he started to come around less, called less, and became very unavailable. I approached him on the subject and he just turned his head, saying, "I've been very busy with schoolwork and haven't had time to see you." I knew that if I pushed him any further he would walk.

Late one night I heard a tap on my door. I jumped down from my top bunk and opened it. Ed stood at the door, asking if he could come in. "Sure," I said. "It's nice to see you." I climbed back on my bunk and he sat on Kathy's bed. As he started to talk, I knew that he was on acid.

"Judy," he said. "I can't handle our relationship anymore. You're too much for me. You think too much and you put a lot of pressure on me. I know that you don't mean to, but you expect me to live up to all your expectations and be everything that no one else has ever been for you. I can't hold up under that."

"Well," I answered. "I'll change for you. I really will. I'll try not to put pressure on you and I'll even stay away for a while."

"No," he said. "It's got to be a lot different from now on. I can't see you anymore."

I jumped off the bunk and stared him in the eyes in unbelief. What had I done wrong? I just didn't understand him at all. I knew that he loved me and cared for me. He went out of his way to show that. I thought of the many hours we had spent walking around campus, or through the woods. I thought about all the nights we had sat up late and talked about our lives. "I don't understand," I said.

And to that he answered, "I have to go. Take care of yourself." Without fighting, I opened the door and let him out. I slammed it as he walked down the hall. I pulled a chair up next to my window and stared at the mountains behind the campus. As cars rode up the country roads I could see their headlights move along the mountain. People walked below me on the campus. My mind went blank.

I walked to my closet and took out some poster paints I had stashed there. Fumbling through my desk drawer, I found a large paintbrush. I walked to my window and started to paint bars on it, making each stroke a little wider. When I finished that work, I walked to the closet and took out a jar of black paint. Across the bars I wrote, "Willis State Hospital."

I stood back and looked at my masterpiece. "It's o.k.," I thought. "But life is really much blacker than that." I walked to the door and began to paint it black from top to bottom. "Life is very much like that," I said, having completed my work.

I walked to my desk and lit two candles. Placing one on my dresser, I proceeded to walk across the room and placed another on Kathy's desk. Turning out the lights, I sat and stared at the flickers on the wall.

"Why doesn't anyone love me?" I thought. "Why doesn't anyone want me?" I mouthed the words as I thought them and tears rolled down my cheeks.

I walked to the window and touched the wet paint. "Is it really that bad?" something inside me asked. "Is it really that horrible?"

"It is," I screamed out loud. "It's a rotten, lousy, unhappy world. And I hate it." I picked up my pillow and started beating it against the wall. "It stinks. Life is lousy," I yelled again. I put down the pillow and walked to my dresser. Taking out a red lipstick, I started to write all over my mirror.

"You are ugly," I wrote. "And no one loves you. No one loves an ugly person. NO ONE CARES!!!"

"Can't you start all over?" I was questioned from within. "Can't you pick up the pieces and try again?"

"I don't know how," I yelled back. "Tell me how!!"

Exhausted, I climbed up on my bed and pulled the covers over my head.

"How does someone believe again when they've lost all faith in life?" I asked myself. "Who do you hold onto as you're pulling yourself up off the ground? Who cares if I live or die? My life is worth nothing!" I blew out the candles and laid my head on the pillow.

I awoke the next morning with Kathy's voice in my ear. "Judy, I need your help. Get up!"

"What's the matter?" I asked.

"It's Carol. She's flipped out. Get dressed and come help me talk her down," she added.

"What happened to her?" I asked.

"She did acid a few nights ago and she never came down. She just wigged out. I think it has to do with the abortion she had. You know how bad she felt about that."

I climbed out of bed, thinking about poor Carol. If anyone deserved the best, it was she. She really tried to do things right.

"Hurry up," Kathy yelled. "She's down in her room and someone has to be with her."

"Has she seen a psychiatrist?" I asked. "Has anyone talked with her?"

"She saw one yesterday and he put her on medication. Brace yourself, because it's pretty gruesome," she added. "You're not going to like what you see."

I pulled on my jeans and T-shirt and followed Kathy down the hall. All the while I wondered how I was going to handle the situation. I had lived through my mother's breakdown, but I didn't know if I could go through another.

We walked down the fire stairs to the fifth floor of the dorm. Looking in Carol's room we saw that she was gone. But, suddenly we heard a scream from the lounge. "I won't die if I jump," I heard Carol say as we entered the lounge. "I won't even get hurt. I'll just bounce right up."

I looked around and saw that there was no one in the room with Carol. She was talking to herself. I walked over to her and put my arms around her.

"How you doing, kid?" I asked, hoping it was the right question. Carol turned and looked me in the face. Kathy stood back, watching for my reaction.

Carol looked me in the eyes and I almost fainted. She had the blank, dead stare of a corpse. It looked as though there were no one behind the eyes. She was rigid and could barely move a muscle. When she'd turned to look at me, only her feet had moved. The rest of her body was stiff and she stood as if she was at attention.

"I'm going to jump," she said to me. "Will you jump with me?" she asked. "We'd bounce back up and climb in the window."

"Carol, you could hurt yourself if you jumped. Why don't we go to your room?" I asked.

A sinister smile came across her face. "What do you know about jumping? What do you know about life?" she asked. "I'm never going to die. But you are. You're going to die. And no one can stop that," she added.

"Come on, Carol," Kathy said. "Let's all of us go to your room. You'll feel better if you sleep for a while." We took her by the arms and dragged her to her room, which she resisted. Her knees did not bend, and she walked like a robot. When we got to her room, Kathy helped her into bed. I stood at the door and held back my screams but not my tears. Carol crawled into bed and then made her body stiff again, as if she were a corpse in a coffin.

"I have to go," I said to Kathy. "I think I need to be alone."

"O.k.," she said. "But will you find Joe and send him down here? I don't want to be alone with her."

"Sure," I said. "I'll send him down."

I walked back to my room, stopping at Joe's to give him the message. "How's she doing?" he asked.

"Not so good," I said, between sniffs. "I've never seen anything like this in my life. Is that what happens to people when they crack up?" I asked.

"Yeah, the doctors say she's a schizophrenic. They say she'll probably never get well."

"I think it's all real sick," I said. "I don't want to be around her. It kills me," I added, as I walked down the hall.

Entering my room, I pulled a chair up next to the window and sat down. "That's how I'll end up," I thought. "I don't have a chance of working out my problems. You can take just so much and then you crack. And there's no way out."

All my life I'd felt that I would crack up just as my mother had. It was my fate and there was no way around it. I'd been fighting it for some time, but I realized that it was time to give up. I was not a winner.

Soon after that, when acid flashbacks came, I did not fight them. I found it harder to keep my mind on reality and started slipping in and out of the real world. The world—life—had a way of stomping all over me and I was tired of the battle. There was no way to win, so I accepted my fate of going crazy. The acceptance of my inevitable insanity brought on a wave of memory blackouts and strange experiences.

One afternoon I found myself standing on the top of a hill just outside campus, screaming and crying. The noise of the wind, rushing through the trees sounded like bass drums and the noise felt as though it would burst my eardrums. I stood beneath the trees, wondering where I was, and ran toward campus in hysteria. I sat on the library steps, trying to calm myself and it was hours before I recognized where I was.

As these blackouts continued, I'd find myself talking with friends and suddenly not know who they were or what we were talking about. My mind drifted off into space, as I dreamed of an escape from life. There was noplace to go physically, so I retreated into a world in my own mind, a place where no one could come and hurt me. A place void of love and life. A tomb.

"I have to kill myself," I thought. "I don't want to be a crazy person. My only choice is death." I walked to my dresser and took out the Valium I'd been prescribed some months before.

As the pills began to take effect and I could feel myself drifting off, a voice penetrated my impending death.

"You're going to hell," it said to me. "And hell is worse than your life here. It's forever."

Panic hit, as I realized that these words were true. I tried to pick myself up and grab for the phone. "I will not go to hell. I don't want to spend eternity there," I mumbled to myself. But, my body was weak from the pills and it took several attempts before I dialed the right number.

"Kathy, I'm dying," I whispered. "Please come save me," I said as the phone fell from my hands to the floor. I fell back and passed out.

I awoke in the emergency room of the Willis Hospital. As I looked up I saw two fuzzy figures above me. "Judy, I'm here." I recognized Dick's voice. Suddenly I felt tubes being pushed down my nose. And I fell off again.

I stayed in the hospital for three days with intravenous tubes in my arms and my body tied to the bed. Friends came and went, offering me gifts and cards. I turned my head toward the wall when they walked into the room. They were trying to "save" me; I didn't want to be saved. I didn't want to go to hell. I'd been given the only choice left. I was going to be a crazy person for the rest of my life.

After my checkout from the hospital, I began my trips to the office of Dr. George, a leading psychiatrist in the area. Feet on desk, he'd say, "Tell me about your relationship with your father." Then he'd cross his arms, waiting for a juicy answer from my shaky, monotonous voice.

I did not know what he wanted me to say. I had no answer for him, so I didn't talk. "Well," he said, "I really want to help you. But if you won't cooperate, I'll have to put you in State."

I'd heard about State. Carol had been shipped there recently. I knew she was probably locked in a room somewhere. She'd never be seen again.

In four months my life had completely fallen apart. I was a

shadow of the person I'd been that August. I couldn't remember who Judy was. Somewhere along the road I'd lost her. She'd been destroyed and taken over by a ruthless force and fate which she couldn't release herself from.

"Think about it," Dr. George said. "I'll see you in three days and we'll make a decision then."

Those days were agony to me. I packed and then unpacked my belongings, not sure if I was going to State or not. I wrestled with the possibility of finding help and getting well. I'd never heard of anyone who went crazy and then got well. Feeling as though everything were a dream, I often pretended that I was not crazy at all. Everyone else was crazy and they'd tried to make me believe that it was me. Someone was playing a big joke with me. Someone had put acid in my orange juice. I wasn't nuts. This just wasn't happening.

But the morning arrived when I had to return to Dr. George's office. I decided it was best to agree with him and tell him what he wanted to hear. "I must cooperate, or else he'll think I really am crazy," I thought.

"Are you willing to try to work things out?" he asked me when I sat down. "You have a lot of work to do and I want to get started."

"I want to get well, but could I see another psychiatrist?" I asked.

"Do you think that would help?" he asked.

"Yes, I think it would."

"O.k., I'll arrange for you to see Dr. Dane, a colleague of mine. But, if you don't cooperate with him, we'll have to put you in State."

"I'll cooperate with him," I said.

Dr. George arranged my first appointment with Dr. Dane and sent me on my way. I hoped Dr. Dane would be a bit more compassionate than Dr. George, whom I hated with all that was within me. He was ruthless and cold.

My first interview with Dr. Dane consisted of filling out forms, giving a family and medical history, talking about my suicide attempt and the fact that I was not responsible for myself.

"I want you to take this medication," he said to me.

"What is it?" I asked.

"Well, there are three kinds—Navane, Cogentin, and Elavil. You'll feel some effects for a while. Your vision will be blurred. You may have muscle twitches. But, the effects will wear off after a while and the medication will help you cope."

"How long do I have to be on it?" I asked.

"Probably for the rest of your life," he said. "I really don't know."

"What's wrong with me?" I asked.

"You've dissociated yourself from life," he said. "And you're paranoid."

"What does that mean?" I asked.

"I hesitate to tell you this, Judy. You've probably read enough psychology to understand what I'm saying. I don't like to label people."

"TELL ME!!" I yelled.

"You're a paranoid schizophrenic," he said. "I don't see that there's much hope of recovery. But you can learn to live with your illness. Many people have done it. The medication will make it easier on you. . . ."

His words stabbed me in the heart. The very thing I had feared had come upon me. He needed say no more. I'd heard all the things they'd said about Carol. And now it was happening to me. There was no need to explain.

"So, I'll learn to live with it," I said. "I'm not sure my family or friends will ever learn to live with it—or understand it. But I'll learn."

I rose to leave, knowing my life had been taken from me. I didn't know why I didn't deserve a happy life. "I really tried," I thought as I walked down the street. "I really tried."

The next morning, I walked to the student union, my local hangout. A woman sat down and shared the Gospel with me. The whole idea of a God who cared for me and wanted to know me personally was far beyond my comprehension. I'd been raised in the Baptist Church, and not once in twelve years had anyone told me that. But this was the era of the "Jesus Freak." Maybe they'd come across something new about God.

I'd done just about everything in life but become a Jesus Freak.
Maybe it was worth a try.

That evening, I sat and prayed. "God, I have really messed
things up. But, I'm not so sure that it has to be this way. I need
to get well. If you can make me well, go ahead and try."

I lay in bed, confessing my sins and repeatedly asking Jesus to
come into my life as Saviour and Lord. I wanted to make sure
He'd heard me, so I asked him several times. Then I closed my
eyes and fell asleep.

7 Believe in Me

I awoke and looked at the room around me. "Kathy?" I said. "Are you here?" There was no answer. The sun was shining through the window. Looking at the clock I realized that it was two o'clock in the afternoon. "I'd better get up," I said to myself, "and get going."

As I climbed off my bunk and dressed, the events of the previous day flashed through my mind. *I had accepted Jesus!!* I thought through my conversation with God the night before. "That's my life, God," I whispered. "If you can put it all together, more power to you."

I walked to the bathroom and washed. I examined myself in the mirror. I didn't look any different. "Isn't there supposed to be a light in my eyes?" I thought, remembering the sparkle in the eyes of the woman who had shared her faith with me. "Well, I guess I can manage without it."

I walked back to my room and picked up the Four Spiritual Laws I'd been given the day before. Turning it over, I noticed a name and address on the back, complete with phone number. The conversation I'd had with the woman flashed through my thoughts. "If you have any questions, please call me," she'd said. "I can't call you," I said out loud. "But I can write you a letter." I sat down on my desk chair and started a note.

"Dear Arlene: I read over the booklet you gave me and decided to accept Christ. I have been looking for something to believe in and maybe this is it. Could you come and pray with me sometime soon?" I signed the letter, addressed an envelope and ran downstairs to mail the letter.

Walking back to my room, I wondered what was next in my life. I felt a little better. There seemed to be a hope I'd never had before. But I wasn't sure what accepting Christ would mean in relation to all the problems I was experiencing. I put the key in my door and entered the room. Walking to the window, I pulled up a chair and sat staring at the mountains behind the campus.

"Judy," I heard a voice within me say, "look around you." I looked around my room, out the window and at the world below me. "You cannot depend on any of these things. They will come and go. But you can depend on me. Learn to trust me."

"How?" I asked out loud. "How do I do that?"

"Trust me and I will show you," the voice answered. "Believe in me and I will heal you."

"I don't know, Jesus," I said. "I don't really know you." I stood up and walked to my closet.

"Look at all the things you have," the voice said. "You have a roof over your head, food to eat, and friends who love you. You will never need more than you have today. But you must believe in me for your healing." I turned around, hoping to see someone standing behind me. No one was there.

"O.k.," I said. "I'll give it all that I have."

I hung up my coat, thinking how funny it seemed to have God talk to me. I could hear His voice so clearly, as it was so different from the confusion and pain I felt on a day to day basis. His words brought peace and conviction, something that was totally new to me. I smiled; I had found a friend.

The next two weeks were the best I'd had in years. I didn't think there was anything in the world that could disturb the peace that surrounded me. I had a new sense of light and life. Where once darkness had penetrated my soul, a new stream of health and warmth entered. "All my problems are solved!" I thought to myself. "And all I have to do now is trust God for the rest." I thought I'd never go back to where I had most recently been emotionally.

I received a phone call from Arlene during those two weeks. "I'll be coming to Willis in a few days. I'd like to come meet with you and pray about God's will for your life," she said.

"Sure," I answered. "I'll be waiting for you."

The day she was to come, I paced my room, wondering if she would really like me and find me lovable. "What if we don't hit it off?" My fear, however, was abated by her presence, which was filled with love and understanding.

"I was ready, at one point of my life," she said, as she sat on the edge of the bed, "to drive my car into a wall. I didn't see any reason for living anymore. That's when I accepted Christ and He gave me a reason to live. And He put all the loose ends of my life together."

"Wow," I thought, "she really does understand how I feel." Taking my hand, Arlene began to pray and her words were full of healing and hope.

"God," she said, "you know Judy better than anyone else in the world. I ask that you'll take her life and make her into the person you want her to be. Put her life together, Jesus, and make her wholly yours." I looked up at her after the "amen" and smiled, so secure in her presence.

Arlene stayed for a while, showing me some Bible studies she wanted me to do in the weeks to come. There was so much that I wanted to tell her about my life, but I couldn't bring myself to start talking. I felt sure that she could not understand all the brokenness within me. So, I buttoned my lips and looked over the studies she was explaining to me. "Read the Bible every day and talk to God as often as you can," she said.

"That sounds easy," I answered. "I shouldn't have a problem with it."

We made an appointment to meet in the next two weeks and she left, assured that I truly belonged to Jesus. I wasn't exactly sure what that meant, and I had a hard time understanding her lingo. The "Christian life" sounded so strange and foreign. What was I supposed to change about myself? I walked around my room practicing "praise the Lord," until it sounded good to my ears.

I quickly told all my friends about my decision to follow Christ. They all looked at me as though I was on "another trip" and would soon give this up, too. But no one seemed shocked or put off by what I'd done. Their response was positive; they were probably hoping I would find answers to my problems.

"Kathy," I asked my roommate one night, "do you believe in God?"

"Sure," she said. "I think He exists."

"Well," I answered, "do you think He can put my life together? Can He make it all better?"

"I don't know," she answered, "but you have nothing to lose by trying."

"Yeah, I guess not," I said. "I've got nothing to lose."

After about two weeks, the wonderful feelings of peace, hope, and new life left. I hit rock bottom. After my close walk with God, my emotional relapse was devastating. The distortion and confusion I had once felt grabbed me by the throat, strangling me.

One evening I was sitting in my room alone, listening to the radio. I was about ready to go to bed, when a wave of fear hit me. I became dizzy and had to grab the bedpost to stand. I sat on the edge of Kathy's bed and suddenly I could feel myself slipping into my other world. "Oh no!!!" I screamed, as I felt myself falling. "Don't let me go, God, don't let me go."

I closed my eyes, hoping the feelings would go away. But, when I opened them, I was in another world. I looked around me. Nothing looked familiar and I didn't know where I was. Suddenly a voice penetrated my fear.

"You're going crazy," it said to me.

"Who are you?" I asked. I looked around the room, trying to find the person who was speaking to me. There was no one there. "My name is Nancy," the voice answered. "And I want you to know that you're going crazy."

"I DON'T KNOW YOU!!" I screamed. "Get out of my room." My mind began to panic as I couldn't figure out where the voice was coming from.

"Leave her alone," another voice piped up. "She isn't going crazy." I listened to this new voice and realized that it was a man. I looked around me again, hoping he would be visible. But, no one was there. "Who are *you?*" I asked.

"My name is Jeffrey, and I'm your friend."

"You are not my friend," I said out loud. "I don't know you either. Why are you bothering me? Make yourself visible."

"We've come to be with you," Jeffrey answered.

"I don't want you here," I screamed. "Go away and leave me alone."

"NO!" he said, almost as if he was insulted. "We won't go away."

I sat on the edge of my bed, trying to find my way back to the other world. But I didn't know how to get back. I wasn't even sure how I had gotten here. I was so lost. All the while Nancy and Jeffrey continued talking to each other, ignoring my pleas that they shut up.

"Who am I?" I asked them. "I don't remember my name."

"Look at your notebook," Nancy said. "Your name is written on the front of it."

I walked to my desk and picked up the notebook. Across the front in black pen was written "Judy Lee." "But, I don't know anyone named Judy Lee," I said to her. "I don't know who she is."

"Well," Nancy said. "It really doesn't matter."

"I want to get out of here," I said. "Please let me out."

"You are free to go," Jeffrey answered. "You can go any time you like."

I walked to the closet and grabbed a coat. Putting it on as quickly as possible, I opened the door and stepped out into the hall. I looked at both ends of the hall. "How did I get in here?" I asked myself. "I don't know how to get out." I walked down the hall until I found an elevator. Pushing the button for the first floor, I fidgeted with my coat, trying to close it. The elevator door opened on the first floor and I walked out, heading for the door. People stopped me along the way and said, "Hi," as I walked right past them. I looked at each person who spoke to me, wondering if I was supposed to know them. They looked familiar but I didn't know who they were.

"Where are you going?" someone asked me as I opened the front door. I kept walking. "Judy!!" I heard someone shout behind me. I didn't look back. Making my way out of the building, I felt a hand on my shoulder. "Judy, where are you going?" a girl asked

me again. I turned around and looked at her. "Judy, are you o.k.?"
she asked.

"Judy?" I thought to myself. "Who is Judy?" I stared at the girl
next to me and tried to talk. "I'm going for a walk. What's it to
you?"

"Well," she answered in a huff, "sorry that I care." She walked
away in disgust.

"Where am I?" I asked myself, as I walked out the door into
the cool air. I didn't know where I was going, but I knew that I
had to get away from *them*—those people who were trying to
drive me crazy. I walked and walked until, exhausted, I sat on a
bench.

I looked at the buildings around me. "This is some lousy trick
they're playing on me," I said to myself. "Someone drugged me
and now they're waiting for me to flip out. Well, I'm not going to
let them get the best of me."

"Judy," I heard a voice within me say. "Judy, I am with you." I
was startled to hear another voice, but as I listened I realized who
it was.

"Jesus, is that you?" I asked.

"Yes, I am with you. Judy, go home."

I sat and listened to God's words. "You are not going crazy.
You are going through a hard time. Don't let go. Don't give up.
Hold onto me, Judy, and I will get you through," He said. As He
spoke, I could feel myself coming back to reality. Jesus was holding my hand and pulling me back through the wall that separated
me from life. After an hour or so of listening to Him, I knew that
I was almost completely back. I dropped my head into my hands
and started to cry.

When I looked up, I recognized that I was on campus—but had
walked far, far away from my dorm. I stood up to start home.

"I have to get back to my room, Jesus," I said. "Help me get
there without flipping out."

"I'm with you," He said, "and I'll take you home." I could feel
Him beside me as I started walking. I was exhausted and drained.
Looking at my watch, I realized that it was six o'clock. I couldn't
remember where I'd been. I didn't know what I had done. "I

hope I didn't do anything crazy," I said to Jesus as we walked across campus. "It's o.k.," He said to me. "You'll be o.k."

I walked back into my room and Kathy was standing beside her dresser. "What the heck was wrong with you this afternoon?" she asked me as I entered.

"What are you talking about?" I asked.

"You know," she said.

"No, I don't," I answered. "I don't have the faintest idea what you're talking about." Kathy stood and looked at me, dropping her hands to her sides.

"Are you taking your medication?" she asked me.

"Yeah," I said, looking at her and trying to figure out what she was getting at.

"When are you seeing Dr. Dane again?" she questioned.

"I have an appointment with him tomorrow afternoon."

Kathy sat on the edge of her bed. "Come here," she said, pointing to the place beside her. I walked over to her and sat down. She put her arm around my shoulder and started to cry. "Judy," she said, "I really don't know what's happening to you. But I want you to know that I love you very much. I worry about you. Is there anything that I can do for you?"

"I don't know," I answered. "I don't understand what's happening to me either. One minute I know where I am, the next I don't." I thought back over the events of the day and started to remember what had happened. I looked at Kathy, wondering if she would understand. "I just forget who I am sometimes, and I don't recognize people I know," I said. "It's really scaring me."

"Well," she answered, "you tell Dr. Dane about it tomorrow. He'll help you."

"Yeah," I answered. "He's pretty nice."

I climbed on my bunk and stared at the ceiling. Closing my eyes, I hoped that tomorrow would come quickly. "Maybe it won't happen again," I assured myself. I tried to believe it wouldn't, but I had no reason to believe that.

My mind was in a daze the next morning. I skipped classes because I was totally drained. The events of the previous day haunted and frightened me. And I knew that at any moment I could slip again into that other world. I sat at my desk and opened my Bible. "I will never fail you nor forsake you." I read. Tears came to my eyes. "I want to believe that," I answered, "but when will I be well?"

I walked into Dr. Dane's office that afternoon, wondering just what I should tell him. He smiled at me as I entered. I wanted so much to please him by getting well right away. It was hard to come to his office week after week, with little change in my life. I thought that he probably hated listening to all my problems. Wishing that I had a funny story to tell him, I said "Hi."

"How was your week?" he asked me.

"Do you want the truth—or do you want me to lie to you?" I asked.

"You don't have to tell me anything you don't want to," he answered. "But I prefer that you don't lie to me."

I hung my head as I recalled to him the story of the previous day. "That's pretty heavy stuff to have to be dealing with," he said. "Have you thought at all about the voices you heard?" he asked me.

"No," I answered. "I don't know what to think about them."

"Maybe you're very lonely and don't like to go through these things alone. That's understandable. Those voices are probably your own thoughts. I think you're talking to yourself!" he said.

I looked up at him and pondered his thoughts. "But why can't I make them go away when I want to? Why don't they leave me alone?" I asked.

"I don't know," he answered. "But I think they are parts of yourself. You must have a lot to say about what's happening to you and this is a way of saying it."

"I suppose," I answered.

"Judy," he said, "have you thought of killing yourself?"

"Not in a while," I answered.

"Do you think of killing anyone else?" he asked.

Shocked, I looked at him again. "NO!!" I said. "I would never do that."

"Well, do you think about it?" he asked again.

"Sometimes the idea of hurting someone back looks good. But, I wouldn't ever do it," I said.

He looked at me and a smile came across his face. "You're

growing," he said to me. "A month ago, all you could think of was killing yourself. I'm proud of you."

I told him about accepting Jesus and how I felt that Jesus was helping me. "You need a lot of help," he said. "And if that helps you, you should stick with it." I looked at him, realizing that he didn't understand that Jesus was a real person. I shut my mouth, wondering if he'd think Jesus was just another one of my delusions.

"Is your medication helping you?" he asked me.

"I don't know," I said. "Things seem to be getting worse and not better. I don't see that it helps."

"It is," he answered. "Let's get you a refill and I'll see you next week." I walked with him to the medicine cabinet and took the pills. A feeling of disgust came over me as I realized that I would be dependent on the medication for the rest of my life. I could not live without it. "It doesn't help at all," I pleaded with him as he walked me to the door. "You need it," he assured me as he turned to walk back to his office.

All during this time, I had not heard from Ed. He had walked out of my life and not even kept in touch. But, through the grapevine, I heard that he was quitting school. I asked Kathy what day he was leaving and she told me.

That morning I sat, waiting for him to come and say good-bye to me. I knew that he would not leave without telling me. I sat all day until the sun set before it sank in that he was never coming back to me. Never, ever.

"God," I said. "Why didn't he even have the decency to come say good-bye. We were good friends. The *best*. I don't understand."

"He doesn't know how to say good-bye," God answered. "He sees all that is happening to you and it frightens him. Don't be angry with him. Let him go." I sat and cried. The only person in the world who I cared about had left me. I didn't know how I could make it through without him around. My last security was gone. I climbed into bed that night believing that he had purposely stabbed me in the heart.

There were days, though, when I would wake up and feel fine. The fear and anxiety would subside and I could try to live a normal life. On days like that, I attended classes, tried to visit my friends, and catch up on life. But, inevitably, fear would strike and I would spin back into my world of confusion and loneliness. There was no way to win the battle.

The hardest thing to cope with was the loneliness. No one understood what was happening to me. Least of all me. I would sit on my bed and talk to Jesus about how I felt, hoping that He would take the feelings away. God was my only strength and comfort. And I was so weak—totally incapable of controlling my thoughts. Often, I'd sit and wonder why God wouldn't miraculously heal me—as I'd heard He'd done for other people. I couldn't understand why I had cracked. Dr. Dane told me that I had experienced a total psychotic breakdown, but I didn't know how one went about pulling oneself back. Even God didn't tell me what to do. I was stuck in a lonely, painful place that I hated.

Sometimes, when I'd slip into the other world, the voices would not come to me. I'd sit on Kathy's bed and pull my knees up to my chest. An awful emptiness would strike at me and I'd close my eyes, hoping, hoping it would go away. There were so many things I had wanted to tell people who came in, but they only looked at me in fear and walked away. It was not hard to forget the look on their faces, as I sat there in the fetal position like a small child. Then I would get up, turn on my small light and open the Bible. All throughout the Scriptures were the words peace, joy, and abundant life. Except for fleeting moments, I didn't have any of those things. I would think about God and wonder how I had failed Him.

"God," I'd ask. "What am I doing wrong? Do I pray enough? Do I read the Bible enough? I don't understand any of this. Your word promises joy." I could sense Him near me and although He did not answer my questions I knew that He was trying to comfort me.

"Judy," He eventually said to me, "I love you the way you are. I do not want you to try to be anyone else. I will heal you and bring you through. But my ways are not your ways. You have to trust me to do it my way."

"I do," I said. "But it just doesn't look very good right now. In fact, it looks awful. Help me believe," I said. And I'd crawl up onto my bunk and cry myself to sleep. I received a letter from Gloria, a girl friend who had written to me about Jesus months before. With the letter was an invitation to come visit her for a weekend. She went to school about 150 miles away. I thought about her invitation and decided it might be good for me to get away for a few days. I called her, making plans to go the next weekend.

All that week, I wondered if I could make it to her place. The blackouts hadn't stopped and I never knew when they'd hit me. But, trying to trust God to get me through, I decided to go.

When I arrived on her campus, and found her dorm, she hugged me and told me that she had made plans to visit a Christian commune fifty miles away the next day. "Will you drive us down there?" she asked me. "It's really a neat place and you'd probably like it." Knowing that she knew nothing about my problems, I cringed as I said "yes." The next day we packed some sandwiches and headed for the interstate.

Driving along, I tried to talk about God. I had such a fear of having a passenger in my car—not knowing when I'd have a blackout. As I tried to suppress my fears, they became worse. And slowly, I felt myself slipping into the other world. In the background I could hear Gloria talking to me, and I could hear myself answering her. But I wasn't "there."

My other world came into view and with that, my voices. "You must drive this car into a wall," Nancy said to me, in an angry tone of voice. "You aren't a human you know. I don't know who ever told you that you were, but they were wrong. You are a Martian and your job on earth is to kill yourself. Look at your hands. They aren't human flesh. *Look at them!!*"

I looked down at my hands and the flesh did not look human to me. "You're right," I said to her in my mind. "What do I have to do?"

I saw an underpass up ahead. As I drove closer, Nancy began to speak again. "You have to drive into that wall," she said. I looked at my speedometer and noticed that I was going sixty miles an hour.

"That ought to do the job," I said to myself. "We'll never know what hit us."

As I drove toward the underpass, a voice came to me. "Don't do it, Judy," it said to me. "Don't do it." I recognized the voice. It was Jesus. "You *don't have to do it*, Judy," He said to me. "I am with you and everything is going to be all right."

I suddenly snapped back to reality and found that I could not turn the wheel toward the side of the road. I couldn't move my hands at all and as I drove under the overpass, I started to cry.

"What's wrong?" Gloria asked, totally unaware of what had happened.

I looked at her through the corner of my eye, trying to form a sentence in my mind. "Oh, I just get sad sometimes," I said. "And it helps me if I cry."

"Well," she answered. "Just remember that Jesus is with you. He will take away your sadness." I looked at her again and smiled. "Sure," I said.

I drove home that Sunday evening in sheer terror. "I have no control at all," I thought to myself. "And there's no telling what's going to happen next." I looked at the road before me and wondered how I could survive.

"Why can't I have a life?" I shouted at God. "Why do I have to be like this? Everyone I know is normal. But not me. I'm tired of being like this. I'm tired of being sick. I want to be well!!" I shouted.

"I love you, Judy," He answered. "And I *am* making you well. You must continue to trust me. I would never let you down. I am always with you and I will pull you through," He said.

"Why do I have to wait?" I shouted in anger. "WHY? All the other Christians I know are happy. They smile, they live a good life. And they don't have the problems I have. Why do I have to be different?"

"Do you love me?" He asked me.

"Yes, I do," I answered.

"Then trust me and I will make you well."

Back on campus, I gradually became aware of the fact that my grades were on the decline. It was hard for me to go to classes, concentrate on what my profs were saying, and then do my work. I was a sociology major and had two hundred to two hundred and fifty pages of reading a week. Sometimes I would sit and try to

study, but I couldn't make my mind stay on any subject longer
than a few minutes. I wanted to do well and graduate. But it
didn't look possible. The fear of flunking out hung over my head.

I was also trying to maintain my friendships. I knew that my
friends loved and cared for me. I was still spending time with
Dick because I knew that I could trust him. And sometimes I
went to visit Arlene for weekends, just to get away and be around
some Christians. But I didn't feel close to any of them. I felt like
a stranger in a strange land. Being around Christians made me
feel lonelier. I had nothing in common with them.

One weekend I went to visit Arlene. She was on staff for Campus Crusade for Christ and was giving a pajama party for some of
the girls she worked with. When I arrived, she was happy to see
me, but I walked into her house feeling very uncomfortable
around all these new people.

"I want you to meet some of my friends," she said to me. And
she began to walk me around the house, introducing me to many
of the girls already there. I looked at them and I wanted to run
away. They weren't my kind.

They all dressed so well, in wool pants, nice blouses and
sweaters. I wore an old pair of blue jeans and a T-shirt—all that I
could afford. As I passed by each group, I listened to their conversations.

"Jesus helped me get a 3.0 this semester. I had such a hard time
pulling good grades before I became a Christian. It seems so easy
now," one girl said.

"I know what you mean," another said. "Before I became a
Christian I used to be so depressed. But, I just don't get depressed
anymore." I looked down at these two girls talking and I wanted
to run upstairs and vomit.

"What is wrong with ME?" I asked myself. "Why don't I have
those kinds of victories in my life?" I excused myself and ran to
Arlene's room and threw myself on her bed. I couldn't hold back
the tears.

"What's wrong?" Arlene asked as she followed me into the
room. "I was talking to you one minute and the next you were
gone." I looked at her for a moment, wondering if she would understand the things I felt. I didn't think that she would. I knew

that I would win no awards in Christian circles for my walk with God.

"Oh, I'm just not used to meeting new people," I said. "It's hard for me."

"Let's pray," she said. We bowed our heads and talked with God. "Help Judy to feel comfortable around these girls. And please, God, forgive her for doubting you."

I opened my eyes and looked at her. "What was she talking about?" I asked myself. "She thinks I have a problem with doubt." I tried to suppress my anger and counteract her prayer with a silent one of my own.

"God, you know that I try to trust you. You know that I can do no more than I am doing. But I am a failure. Look at all those other people down there. I will never be like them. They have 'the victory.' And God, if I ever get the victory, please don't let me be like them. Don't ever let me be so shallow."

"Amen," Arlene said. "Don't you feel better?"

I stared at her for a moment, wondering if I should set her straight. I knew that my words would be wasted.

"Sure," I said. "Let's go."

8 Yea, Though I Walk Through the Valley....

The school year ended quickly, and much to my dismay, I had to return home for the summer. Anne, my oldest sister, had offered me a room at her house. I planned on getting a job and working to save money for school the next fall.

I drove home, wondering if I could hold a job and make it through the summer. I didn't like to be around my family because they had never come to terms with my problems. Instead of understanding, or acknowledging the things I struggled with, they denied them. It left me feeling very much alone. I prayed all the way home that God would give me the strength to deal with the family all summer, and the patience to be kind no matter how I felt about them.

I settled at my sister's and went out to find work. I was lucky to find a waitress position at a local restaurant. I started just a few days after I arrived, working the dinner shift. But after only a couple of days on the job, I knew that I did not have the stamina, mental strength, or perseverence to hold the job. Often, I would lose my train of thought and forget where I was. Other times my whole body would begin to shake, in fear that I'd make a mistake. I became such an emotional wreck that I had to quit the job after a few weeks. I could not go on.

The summer passed uneventfully, my mind always in another world. Sometimes I would be able to pull myself back, but I had

given up fighting my symptoms. The medication had finally
begun to help me. It calmed me down some and drowned out
many of my emotions. I could function and survive, but it was at
the lowest level of existence. I was merely alive, but unable to
function as a normal person.

That fall I returned to school with an attitude of defeat. Kathy
had not asked me to live with her that year, so I was assigned a
room with a girl I didn't know. It didn't matter to me. Nothing
mattered. I believed that I was stuck forever in the illness that
had gripped my life. I had no desire to kick back or get out of
sorts about anything. Thoroughly convinced that nothing mattered, I slipped into the stream of life, and pretended that I had
everything under control.

"Hi, my name is Rona," my new roommate said to me as I
walked into the room. I looked at her, studying her from head to
foot. Then I put my things down. "My name is Judy," I said.
"And I'm a paranoid schizophrenic." Rona looked at me and
turned away.

"Well," I said to myself, "I'd better prepare her for the worst.
It's good that she knows right from the start that I'm crazy." I
looked at her across the room as she pretended that she hadn't
heard that. I laughed to myself. "No one understands," I thought.
"And they probably never will."

I started to unpack my things. Coming across my Bible, I threw
it on my desk. "Are you a Christian?" Rona asked.

"No," I said. "I'm a Christian paranoid schizophrenic. There's a
difference, you know. Christians lead happy lives. Christian paranoid schizophrenics lead very unhappy and dreary lives. I'm not
into labels myself. I prefer to call myself a person."

"I'm a Christian, too," she said. "I haven't been to church in a
while and I seldom read the Bible. But, I accepted the Lord a few
years ago."

I looked at her to see if she was serious. Did I have a fanatic on
my hands—all smiles and roses? I sized her up and decided not.
"Don't mess with God," I said. "If you're going to walk with
Him, get serious. If not, get out of His way." I explained to her
what carnal Christians were. "I think you're in that group," I said,
"but far be it for me to judge. I don't care what your relationship

with God is, just so long as you don't get on my case." Rona
smiled and I knew that she understood what I was talking about.

Classes started and I tried to throw myself into my work. But
having lost interest in all things around me, I could not really put
my heart into anything. I had resigned myself to being hopelessly
sick forever. I would slide through as best I could and not hope
for the best. School was one of the things I had to "get through,"
so I was putting out only what I had to. Besides that, I had little
energy to study or do anything else. My heart was in the right
place, I desired to do well, but my mind and body would not cooperate.

I sat one day on my bed, thinking about how I was going to
handle all the new things in my life. I was planning my conversations, the things I would say to people, the way I would act and
appear. I wanted to appear as sane and normal as possible, but it
took a lot of will power and planning. Rona saw me sitting there,
staring at the wall.

"Have you ever thought about pledging a sorority?" she asked.

"Oh, come on," I answered. "That's kid stuff. You're not serious, are you?"

"Yeah, I am," she said. "Want to go around to the different
houses with me? You don't have to pledge if you don't want to.
But come and meet some of the girls and give it a try."

I looked at her as though she were crazy. Then I looked at my
life. I was not the social butterfly I wished I was. My life was not
jam-packed with interesting things to do. "Sure," I said to Rona.
"I'll give it a try."

That evening we went out to look at the different sororities and
see what they had to offer us. I wondered if maybe it wouldn't
help me to get involved with a group of people. I was lonely and
could use a few friends. "But this is no way to make friends," I
thought. I decided that the whole idea was rather silly.

Rona and I made the rounds. Each house was different in the
type of girl they took and how they handled people. One took
only the "good looker," another only the brains. It was not hard
to spot the specialty of every sorority, after spending only a few
minutes in the house. Most of them bored me. But then we came
to Delta Psi.

Unlike every other place we'd been, this house looked like a home. It looked lived-in. People walked around with an ease that I had not seen anywhere else. There were few pretensions in this group of girls, and I thought that rather nice. In listening to conversations around me, I discovered that they were having financial problems and might lose their house. Not many girls wanted to pledge Delta anymore because it had gone downhill socially over the past ten years. It was not a highly respected or recognized house. And this pleased me to no end. For the first time all evening, I felt comfortable.

The next day I put a bid in for Delta and Rona put a bid in for another house. I was sad that she hadn't gone for the same sorority as I had, but I knew that she'd be happier elsewhere. A few hours later we both found out that we had been accepted by the sorority of our choice.

Pledging, the slow process of initiation, began immediately. Delta had only six girls, which was nice, because it gave us a chance to get to know each other. We had to meet every night, for one matter or another and through this process I became close friends with Buddy.

Buddy was a year younger than I, but we had much in common. We shared the same sense of humor, the same cynicism and the same desires. We both hoped for a better life. She was an epileptic, which corresponded with my illness, as far as I was concerned. I liked Buddy and we started hanging out together. Because she was unthreatening and as weak as I was, I felt safe and secure with her.

But as pledging continued, through the weeks, the hopelessness in my life increased. My efforts to make friends and try to find solutions to my problems seemed fruitless. By the end of October I didn't see how I could make it through the whole school year. I was always holding onto the end of my rope, hoping I wouldn't fall, but thinking that I probably would. For weeks on end, I went into depressions that I couldn't break. The only thing different that year from the year before was that I didn't try as hard. It didn't seem to matter. One day I talked to Buddy about it.

"Why don't you go home for a while and rest?" she asked.

"Maybe if you aren't under the pressures of school you can work things out for yourself."

"But, I can't go home, Buddy," I said. "My father doesn't want me and neither does my stepmother. They gave up on me a long time ago. They couldn't be bothered."

"So just try. Call home and see what he has to say," Buddy added.

I rushed to my room and dialed the phone. "Dad," I said, "can I come home for a while?"

"What's the matter with you, Judy? Why can't you stick anything out? Stay in school and get good grades," he said.

"But, Dad, I'm having problems and I need some time to put my life together," I said.

"Look, Judy, you have to help yourself. There's nothing I can do for you," he answered.

I hung up. "Why can't he ever understand me? Why?" I thought back over the many years we had not been able to communicate. "He'll never understand me," I cried. "*Never.*"

Then I remembered my sister Phyllis. She was living on an army base not far away. I picked up the phone to call her. I knew that she would understand what I was going through. "Phyllis, hi, this is Judy."

"How are you doing? I haven't heard from you for a while," she said.

"Phyllis, things aren't good right now. I need to get away and I need to do it soon. Could I come stay with you for a while?" I asked.

"Let me ask Barry when he comes home," she said. "And I'll call you back. What's your number?" I gave her my number and waited for her to call back.

When she returned my call, she said that I could come and stay with her. I was jubilant.

I packed and the next day I went to the administration building to withdraw from school. Then I had to go to the head of the program I was in to make sure that I would be funded if I returned the next semester. I dreaded the conversation I would have with the director of the program. I knew that there was no "reason" to give him for my withdrawal, without explaining the past three years of my life. I didn't have time to do that.

"Judy," he said, "what does a young girl like you have to bother her? You shouldn't have any problems."

"Yeah, I know that I shouldn't have any problems. But I do. And I need time to think some things through. If I come back in January, will there be funding for me?" I asked.

"Call me before Christmas vacation and remind me to hold a spot for you," Dr. Kent said. "And there should be no problems."

I ran from the administration building and packed my car. Just as quickly, I hopped in and started the three-hour drive to my sister's house. My mind wandered in and out of reality. The change in worlds was not so drastic anymore. The medication had taken the edge off the transition from one world to another. And I accepted, weeks before, this drifting in and out of different spheres. It had become, to me, a way of life, a routine and a structure I could depend on. I did not find it frightening that day to find myself slipping from world to world.

I stayed at Phyllis's house for only two weeks. Living with her did not solve my problems, something I had hoped it would. I was looking for immediate solutions and was willing to try anything to make my problems go away. Everything around me was to blame for the things I was going through. Many times I thought through my family problems. I could think back and remember where things had been wrong. But I didn't know how to put them right. I returned to school, knowing I had nowhere else to go, and hoping I'd find a place to live until the next semester started.

I stopped, first, at the sorority house, believing they would put me up for a while. But, upon arriving, I discovered that they had no room and couldn't let me stay there. I felt like a burden to everyone around me and I didn't know where to turn. So, I tried calling my father again.

"Well, you might as well come home," he said to me. "You have to live somewhere. But, I want you to know that I don't like the idea and I think you are acting very immaturely. You have to grow up sometime."

"I'll be home tomorrow," I said to him. "And I'll be good. I won't blow it this time."

As I was driving home, I thought about what a child I was. I was totally unable to make it on my own. I felt like a fly in a Plexiglas box. At first, I had tried to fly around and find my way out. But, after a while I had given up. I was tired of beating my head against the sides of the box. Now, I was cowered in the corner, my head drooped and my will broken. Adjusting to and structuring my life around my symptoms seemed the only way to survive. "I'm just a kid," I thought to myself. "And I'll never be an adult."

Upon arriving home, I was able to secure a job at a local factory. I was lucky, also, to find a good Christian fellowship—something I had not had the past year and a half at school. I threw myself into both those things and within two weeks, my life began to improve.

Living at home also made me feel secure. I had a family around me that I could talk to, share with and do things with. There was not much time to be alone and think about all my problems. A sense of peace came over me and slowly the craziness began to disappear. I was shocked at this turn of events. I did not understand why I should suddenly, at this time, find peace and rest from the battle I had fought for so long. I realize now that it was because many of my needs were being met. For the first time in my life, I felt like I was in the right place, doing the right things. But, I didn't know what I was doing right. All I knew was that I felt well for the first time in a year and a half.

I felt so good, in fact, that I made plans to return to school in January, thinking that I had solved all my problems and could now lead a normal life.

But in January, the moment I drove on campus the awful confusion and depression hit me again. I couldn't believe it. All my symptoms returned and I knew that I was defeated. I called Dr. Dane as soon as I was settled in my room, hoping that he had some answers for me.

"Judy," he said, "you have a lot of problems. It will take years to even begin to sort them out. I don't think you should expect much of yourself. You have to learn to take it a day at a time. And you have progressed some since I first saw you. But you have a long way to go. Learn to cope with your illness until we find out what it is that bothers you so much."

That was the last thing in the world I wanted to hear. I was so full of anger and disappointment that I wanted to scream. I looked at the world around me and I looked at Christianity. It was all a sham. God had no power to make me well. Why had He told me that He would? He had no power to change me. I was sick of hearing His promises.

And I hated Christians. I hated them because they had all the things I didn't have, but wanted. They had life and happiness, peace and joy. None of these things were mine, and they never would be. I was a bad person. I had failed God in some way, and this was my punishment.

I was so discouraged and angry at Him that I never wanted to hear from Him again. Either He was going to put my life together, or He was going to get out of my life. I was tired of walking the middle of the road, hoping against hope, believing and trusting when I had no reason to. I was so tired of God and so disgusted with smiling Christians that they made me sick. So, I again decided to give up.

I contacted Buddy soon after I'd seen Dr. Dane. She was into partying, so I joined her in the evening and began to live my old life style. I just couldn't see that it made any difference whether I drank, partied, stayed out late at night or not. Either way, I was still sick and all I wanted was healing. Since that healing had not come, I wanted to escape my problems. Staying out, night after night with Buddy, was the perfect way.

I also stayed as far away from Arlene as possible. Sometimes she would call or drop in when she was on campus, but I tried to avoid her when I could. I began to make excuses when I knew she'd be around and went my own way.

Often she would tell me that I was the one who was a carnal Christian. I wondered if I was a carnal Christian by choice or by force. I had lost respect for much of what she said. I was tired of being told to trust God and hold onto Him. That was not my answer. She could talk all the right religious things, but when it came down to how I could get well, she had no answers. I completely gave up on her and decided that she was out in left field somewhere, totally out of contact with reality.

I could not help but be bitter. I had tried to live a righteous life, hadn't I? I could not see how my going out drinking and partying could be any worse than the inconsistencies I saw in other Christians. Dishonesty, to me, was the worst sin there was. And dishonesty in believers was the major factor in my bitterness. My sin was no worse than theirs and I didn't believe that anyone had a right to point the finger at me. I *could not* fit into their role for me—smiling all the time and saying things were all right when they weren't.

God knew what I was doing. I was not trying to hide my life from Him. Often, I told Him that I did not want to drink, but I couldn't handle the pressures I was under and I could find no way of eliminating them. If a solution had come, I would have given up my partying in a moment. But, most of all, God knew whether I was a carnal Christian or not. That was His judgment to make, not someone else's. I was no longer going to pretend that life with God was the ultimate solution to every problem in life. It was not. Accepting Christ had not zapped away my illness, it had only made it tolerable. And I knew that God understood that. I also knew that there was nothing more I could do for my life until He made a move. There was no choice but to make myself as comfortable as possible until He did something.

The school year drew to a close, many of the months behind me just a blur. From day to day I could not remember what I had done or where I had been. My mind was in the process of wiping all memories out of sight, so I would not have to look at the horror of my life. I knew that school was ending, but I wondered where I'd been for so many months.

I knew that I couldn't go home. I had flunked two semesters in a row and the director of the program I was in wanted me to go to summer school and get my grades up. If I didn't get them up, there would be no money for me in the fall.

Buddy also had to attend summer school. She wanted to graduate early so she could go on to med school. We both made plans to move into the sorority house and room together. The last day of school I helped her move her things in.

My first week there, I wrote a check for a hundred dollars for rent. A week later I got a notice from my bank at home that it had bounced. I ran upstairs and looked at my checkbook. My records showed that I had over two hundred dollars in my account. I rushed to call the bank and clear up the problem.

"You are overdrawn for over one hundred dollars," the man on the other end told me.

"That's impossible," I said. "I have been sending you checks all along and my records show that I have money in my account."

"Send us a copy of your receipts," he said to me. "And I'll clear this up for you."

I rummaged through my things and discovered that in the process of moving my receipts had been lost. There was no way I could prove that I had money in my account. I knew that I would have to quit school and work. In the meantime, I needed money and decided to call my father and see if he would help me out.

"I want you to come home," he said to me. "Borrow money from someone, but make sure that you are here tomorrow afternoon." I hung up, wondering why he was on my case. "What have I done wrong now?" I thought.

I borrowed money from Buddy and flew home the next day. My brother picked me up at the airport. "You're in big trouble," he said to me. "You really blew it this time."

"What did I do?" I asked him.

"Just wait," he answered. "You'll find out."

When I got to my father's house, he called me from his office. "Get down here right away," he said. "I want to talk to you."

I borrowed my stepmother's car and drove to his place of business. He was standing on the doorstep waiting for me.

"I got your grades in the mail," he said, "and you flunked."

"You have no right to open my mail," I said to him. "And it's none of your business if I fail or not."

"It is my business," he said. "You have failed and failed. When are you going to grow up and become an adult? I have tried to help you, over and over again. But you won't act like an adult. I'll help you clear up this bank mess you're in and then that's it. I will give you no more and I don't want to see you until you grow

up. Don't ask me for anything else. And don't come home until
you get your life together."

I looked at him aghast. My grades were the least of my problems. Money was only a small part of my needs. "How can he be
so cruel as to overlook all the emotional problems I have?" I asked
myself. "That's fine with me. I don't need you and I can make it
on my own," I said as I walked out of the room.

I flew back to Willis that evening, thinking over the conversation. I was at a loss for words to explain how I felt. My family
knew of my problems yet they denied them because they didn't
know how to deal with them. In that, they wiped out my existence. I was only a problem to them. The plane landed and my
mind turned to the things that faced me now, in the present.

I had no money and had to find a job. I talked with Dr. Dane
during my next appointment and he suggested that I go on welfare. I drove to the welfare office soon after to sign up. They had
no jobs available, so they took all the information they needed
from me and told me they'd send me a check—$127 a month to
live on. I had car insurance due—$60 that month. I had rent
due—$60 that month. And that left me with only $7 for food and
miscellaneous items for the rest of the month. I lived, during that
time, on chicken noodle soup and concentration cereal—except
during times when other girls would invite me to eat with them.

A week later, welfare called me in for a job interview. One of the
local Catholic churches needed someone to clean the convent. I
didn't have any dressy clothes to wear on the interview, so I went
in blue jeans and an Indian top. It is not surprising that I didn't
get the job.

The priest who interviewed me thought that I was pregnant. I
had gained thirty pounds in the past year and the Indian top I
wore made me look suspect. He called the welfare office and told
them that I was. They, in turn, called me and threatened to cut
off my check. I told them that I wasn't pregnant but they
wouldn't believe me. Finally I gave them Dr. Dane's number and
asked them to call him to confirm my story. This incident was yet
another blow to my self-esteem.

I was sincerely looking for a way to find a job and get out of the
rut I was in. One of the girls in the sorority house mentioned a

secretarial school that offered a ten-week course for people who had a college background. "It'll give you the skills you need to find a good job," she said. "And it would get you off welfare."

These were magic words to me. I prayed about the possibility of going and believed that God wanted me to do that. The course cost four hundred dollars and I didn't know where the money could come from. In desperation I called my father and asked him if he would help me. "It's only four hundred dollars, Dad, and then I could get a job and go to work."

"You could work if you wanted to. There are always jobs around. You just don't want to work because you're lazy," he said. "I won't help you."

That was, for me, the final and crushing blow. I could take no more. I had been biding my time, waiting for God to help me, waiting for healing to come. I had done all the things I believed I'd had to do. I had done all that I could. And now everyone was bailing out on me. Everything had failed. And I knew that I could not go out.

Without much thought on the matter, I walked to the kitchen and took out a large carving knife. Then I snuck into the cellar to find a hose. I cut a long piece off and headed to my car.

Taking one end of the hose, I pushed it into the exhaust pipe. The other I slipped into the passenger side window. I climbed into my car, rolled up all the windows and turned on the car.

"I don't have to live like this anymore," I told myself. "I don't want to be half a person."

Meanwhile, Buddy had felt an uncontrollable urge to find me, sensing that something was wrong. She searched all throughout the house for me. Then she heard me start my car. Grabbing another girl by the arm, she came running out to see what I was doing and saw the hose.

Running to the passenger side, she pulled the hose out of the window and began to speak to me. She put her hand on the door-knob, thinking she'd climb in and talk.

I grabbed the knife next to me and pointed it at her. "Don't you come near me," I said. "You have no right to tell me that I have to live. You don't have to live the way I do. So, you're an epileptic. At least you're sane. I'm not sane. I cannot control my

thoughts and I can't live a normal life. No one understands me. I
have no reason to live. Get away from me or I'll kill you."

Buddy looked at me in shock, knowing that I was serious.
"Judy, I really love you. Please don't kill yourself. I'll miss you.
You're the only friend I have, and if you die, I won't have anyone.
There'll be no one left. Please come inside," she said.

Her words had a soothing effect on me. It was the first time in
many moons I had heard someone say that they needed me. I
looked at her. "Do you really need me?" I asked. "Do you really
need me?"

"Yes, I do. I do very much," she answered.

"O.k.," I said, "I'll come inside."

Buddy put her arm around me as we walked to the house. Then
she walked me to our room and sat on the edge of the bed as I
cried my heart out. God had been faithful, even when I had not
been and He had again saved me from myself.

The next day I had an appointment with Dr. Dane. I knew
that I had to tell him about the night before. But I was sure that
he would be so angry with me that he'd put me away in the state
hospital. I really didn't care, at this point, what he did. I was almost happy at the thought of going away forever. I began my conversation with him, for the first time since I had known him, with
little fear of his power over me.

"I tried to kill myself, you know," I said to him. "If you can
give me a good reason to go on living, then tell me. If not, don't
get on my case."

"What's bugging you?" he asked, almost ignoring my bellig-
erence. "Well, I want to go to secretarial school and I don't have
any money. If I don't go, I'll never get off welfare and I'll always
be a failure."

"Do you think you can handle secretarial school?" he asked.

"Well, it's only for ten weeks. I think I could get through it," I
answered.

"Do you think you could handle a job full time?" he asked
again.

"I don't have a choice, do I?" I answered. "It's either a job or a
hospital. I'm willing to take my risks on the outside. I think that I
could learn to handle it."

"Well, I know of a program that might be able to give you the money to go. I can't promise you that they will, but I can call and try to set up an appointment for you," he said.

"Would you really do that for me?" I asked.

"Yes, I would. I would have done it sooner if I had thought that you were really serious about going to secretarial school. I didn't know that you wanted to go so badly," he said. "I'll give you a call when I find out whether or not they can help you."

I drove home, thinking that maybe there was hope after all. A few days later Dr. Dane called me and asked me to come in that afternoon for an interview with a counselor in the program. I rushed over and sat to answer her questions. Then I went home, praying all the way, and for the next five days, that God would open this door for me.

And then Dr. Dane called. "Judy, I have good news for you. The program is going to fund you. You can go to secretarial school."

"Thank God!" It was the *first* ray of hope I had had in a year. "God really knows that I'm alive," I said to myself. "He really does love me."

I sat and cried as all the doubt and anger that had built over the past year began to dissolve.

9 There Is a Time to Cry

The idea of leaving Willis was a rush to my system. There had been no solid Christian fellowship for me, nothing that interested me, and I had felt completely supportless. But now I could see the light at the end of the tunnel—a future and a job.

But, after being accepted at secretarial school and having my funding arranged, I realized that I had nowhere to live. I had no place to go, so I called Arlene, hoping she knew of someone who would rent me a room.

"Hi, Judy," she said. "I've been thinking of you the past few days. How are you doing?"

"I'm o.k.," I said as I explained my plan to move to Andor. "But, I don't have a place to live. Do you know anyone I could stay with—maybe a family or some girls?"

"Well," she said, "there's a group of Christian girls who have a house not far from my place. I don't know if it is filled for next semester. Do you want me to check?" she asked.

"Do you know of anything else?" I questioned.

"No, not offhand. But, I can call one of the girls and see if they'd have a room for you. Let me try now and I'll call you back," she said.

I hung up wondering how living with a group of Christians would work out. I had found it hard to relate to those I had met so far. I found them to be a peculiar group of people. Lighthearted and happy, they always seemed to have it together. I, however, was always on the other end of the stick. I hadn't even begun to experience the "victorious Christian life" and wasn't sure that I ever would.

Arlene returned my call a few hours later. I was surprised to hear from her so quickly, but she was excited to tell me what she had learned.

"The girls have one room left—available at the end of the summer. From what they tell me, the house is pretty big. You'd have privacy and space of your own," she said. "I know some of the girls—they're members of Crusade. And they're pretty nice. In fact, you may have met some of them."

"What's the rent?" I asked, calculating my welfare payment in my head.

"Seventy-five dollars a month. The girls each give ten dollars a week for food. Electric is a little extra and I think they have to pay for their heat. Could you afford that?" she asked.

"I guess I could. Welfare will just have to give me more than I get now," I said, wondering how that was possible.

"Do you want me to call them and tell them you're coming?" she asked. "They need to know right away."

"Yeah," I answered. "Give them a call. Do you have their phone number and address?" I asked. "I'll probably move in the end of August and I don't know how to reach them."

Arlene gave me the information and promised to firm things up with the girls that very afternoon. The rest was up to me. I had to show up. And I wondered how I was going to handle it. I had talked to Buddy many times about my move and I turned to her again for support.

"Judy, I think it's great that you're going. You need to get out of here. But, I have good news for you," she added. "I'm going home at the end of the summer. I don't have the money to continue school."

"So, what good does that do me?" I asked. "You don't live in Andor."

"No, but I live in Clyde and it's only five miles from Andor," she said.

"Are you serious?" I asked. "Are you for real?"

"Yup," she said. "And we could get together on weekends and do things. You're not going alone."

I smiled. "Funny, how God doesn't desert us," I thought to myself. I realized that I had learned more about God's faithfulness in the past few weeks than I had in two years.

But the last few weeks before moving to Andor were very hard for me. I was leaving what had been my home for three years. And it was more like home than the town I'd grown up in. Also, I was leaving Dr. Dane. I had been seeing him for two years now and he was my last earthly hold on sanity. He knew me inside out and upside down. I trusted him and believed in him. Also, I was putting my college education behind me—my dreams of graduating had been shattered. And there was doubt in my mind as to whether or not I'd ever see all my friends again.

I knew in my heart that this was the way it should be. I had to look forward and not back. Stepping out in faith was not one of my strong points. I was like a child who had been frightened by lightning and refused to come out from beneath the bed. And all by myself, I had to crawl out, face my fears, and go on. I could do nothing but cry as I said my good-byes and sent my new address to all my friends who were home for the summer. Those tears brought a certain death to one stage of my life. But I clung to the hope of a new life ahead of me.

My day of departure arrived and I packed my things and stuffed them all into my VW Bug. The drive took only an hour and a half, but it seemed like forever. I slipped in and out of reality all the way there—a part of me refusing to leave. I tried to push it aside and go on, but it would not obey me.

Finally, I pulled up in front of "the house"—a large structure which hadn't been painted in years. The roof was sinking in the front and the lawn was overgrown. I turned off the ignition and made my way to the door, hoping I was having a bad dream, but knowing that I wasn't. Clearing my throat, I rang the bell and stood in fear as I waited for someone to answer.

The girl who answered the door stood and stared at me. "Hi," I said, trying to be cheerful. "My name is Judy and I've come to live here."

"I don't know anything about that," she answered. "No one told me that you were coming."

I looked at her for a minute, my eyes pleading with her to remember my name. "Do you know Arlene?" I asked, not knowing where to begin. "She's the one who arranged for me to live here."

"I know her, but I really didn't expect you. No one told me . . ." she said, as she let me in the door. "But you can have this room until I straighten this out," she said, pointing to a small room off the foyer. "It needs to be cleaned. The girls are away for the summer and no one has fixed it up. But, it's a nice room." I opened the door and looked in. "It will do," I said, as I headed back toward the door to get my things from my car.

"Do you need any help?" she asked me. "By the way, my name is Debbie," she added as she followed me out the door.

After getting settled, I made my way to the kitchen and found her cooking some soup. "Do you know where the welfare office is?" I asked, explaining my financial arrangements. "I have to switch my case to this county so I can get my checks."

"Yeah, it's down on State Street," she said, explaining how I could get there. I listened, wrote down her directions and thanked her for her help, making a mental note to stop in there first thing the next day.

I walked around the house for a while, checking out the different rooms. The house was dark and musty, a dreary sort of place that cried out for light and color. Climbing to the third floor, I discovered a cute little studio that was completely cut off from the rest of the house. I wished I could live there, but since I hadn't been offered the space, I kept my peace. Finally, I made my way downstairs and turned on the TV, for lack of anything else to do.

The next morning, I made my way to the welfare office, thinking the process of changing residence would take but an hour or so. I was surprised to find myself sitting hour after hour before my name was called. The sitting was tedious and I studied everything around me in great detail.

Most everyone looked very poor. Some women sat with two or three small children around them. Young men in dirty, torn clothes sat with their heads drooped, waiting for their names to be called. The walls of the office were institutional blue, filthy from the many fingerprints and smudges left by previous clients.

The place smelled of poverty and a definite lack of dignity. I wanted to get up and run out, asking myself all the while how I had ended up with this crowd of people. The longer I waited, the lower my self-esteem became. When finally my turn came to be interviewed, I felt exactly the way everyone around me looked. And I was willing to do anything to get a check and get out of there. The waiting and watching had reduced me to a shell of a human being.

After filling out the multitude of forms and being assured of a check, I ran to my car and drove home. It looked even more dreary to me than it had the day before. And, I had nothing to do. My mind in a panic, I wondered how I would fill the next few weeks until school started. And then I remembered Ann.

I didn't know if she was home for the summer or still here in town. I hadn't seen or talked to her in so long that I didn't even have an address for her. Picking up the phone, I dialed her mother and asked for her phone number and address. Just as quickly, I hung up and dialed her local number. After only one ring, Ann picked up.

"Ann?" I asked. "This is Judy."

"Well, where have you been?" she asked. "I haven't seen you in ages."

"I've just moved to Andor. Can I come see you?"

"Sure," she said, and she gave me directions to her house.

I drove there, thinking that she was my only real friend in town. I had grown up with her and all my life she had been like a sister to me. There was nothing we hadn't shared. And I wondered if I would be able to now pick up where we had left off.

I knocked on her door. Answering the door, she stood with a joint of grass in her hand. "Want to smoke?" she asked as she let me in.

"I don't do that anymore," I said. "I gave it up."

"So what's been happening?" she asked, as she pointed to a chair in the living room. "I heard that you became a Jesus Freak."

"Things sure get around," I said. I began to tell her of my conversion and all the things that had happened to me since our last meeting. She sat and smiled at me as I explained my breakdown and my attempt to put my life together.

"You want a drink?" she asked me.

"Isn't it a little early in the day for that?" I asked. "What have you been doing?" I asked, knowing that she wanted to change the subject.

"Well, I've mostly been dealing drugs this past year. Roy lives with me and we make good money. I flunked out of college last year and my parents are really upset with me," she said. "But, I don't care. I have what I want and I don't need them."

"Not until you need money," I said. And then I reminded her of the many times she had run home to Mommy and Daddy for a couple hundred bucks. "You use them, Ann," I said. "And I think it's crummy."

"Well, they have the bucks and they think they're doing a good thing for me. I take what I can get, where I can get it, and I don't argue," she said.

"Are you working?" I asked, hoping she had not completely dropped out of life.

"No, not really. I work as a go-go dancer once in a while. But, when drug sales are up, I don't have to work," she said.

I sat staring at her to see if she could look me in the eye. "Ann, don't you think there's a better way to get through life?" I asked. "You're going to get in trouble."

"Not me," she said. "I'm too smart and so is Roy."

"Well, look," I said. "I have to go. Let's keep in touch." I gave her my phone number and address. "Call me once in a while. You're the only one I know in town. Will you call me?" I asked.

"Sure, Jude! Talk to you soon," she said, as I made my way to the door. "I'll call you soon."

Hopping into my car and driving away, I thought about Ann. "She'll probably get busted," I thought to myself. "She doesn't have enough brains to keep her mouth shut." I considered her whole situation rather hopeless. And it saddened me to see what she had done with her life. There was so much potential—and she had thrown it all out the window. But, I couldn't help but love and care for her. The years we had spent together were not easily erased by this twist in events.

Buddy moved home a week early and called to surprise me. "Want to go for a ride?" she asked when I picked up the phone. "I don't have anything to do tonight and I thought you might want to get together."

"Sure," I answered. "You don't know what a lifesaver you are. I've been going crazy trying to find something to do. When should I pick you up?" I asked.

"At eight o'clock," Buddy answered, explaining how I could get to her house. "I can't wait to see you."

I couldn't wait to see her. Buddy was special to me. Although she was not a Christian, I could tell her the deepest things in my heart. She encouraged me to follow Christ and keep the faith. And she made no demands of me. She liked and accepted me just as I was. I drove to her house, a sense of relief coming over me.

When she opened the door, I jumped out of my car and ran up to throw my arms around her. I dragged her to my car and told her about my new life. "Buddy, things aren't so good for me. My mind is going blank and I can't think," I said. "I feel just like I did before I had the breakdown."

"You don't look so good," she answered, studying my face. "You look a little spaced out. Have you been sleeping at night?"

"Not really," I answered. "My mind goes over and over so many things. The girls in the house where I'm living will be here soon for the fall semester. I don't think I want to live there, Buddy. I'm scared. I can't handle all this change and keep my head at the same time!" I cried.

"Sounds like you need some help. Are you seeing a psychiatrist in town?" she asked.

"I don't know who to see or where to go," I said. "I don't know this city."

"Well, there's a state psychiatric hospital not far from where you live. Why don't you call them in the morning? I'm sure they could set up an appointment for you. Will you promise me you'll do that?" she asked.

"Yeah, I will. Buddy, will you love me no matter what happens to me? If I crack up, will you come visit me?" I asked.

"Sure," she answered. "And if I have to live at home for too long with my mother I may have to join you."

"Maybe they have a 'buddy' system," I joked. "And we could go as a team." Having broken the ice, I turned the conversation to other things and we spent the night discussing our lives and our fears.

Upon returning home, my mind returned to my earlier conversation with Buddy. I looked at myself in the mirror. I had gained fifty pounds since high school, mostly from the medication I'd been taking for the past two years. My face was puffy and my eyes were like slits. "You're a zombie," I screamed at myself. "You don't even look like the same person anymore. I don't know you," I yelled. I climbed into bed, hating myself and the world around me.

But the next morning I awoke remembering to call the psychiatric hospital. I looked up the number in the directory and dialed the number. My hand shook as I waited for an answer.

"Hatkins Psychiatric Hospital. Can I help you?" the voice on the other end chimed.

"My name is Judy Lee and I'd like to see one of your psychiatrists," I said. "Can you arrange that?"

"Just a moment and I'll connect you," she answered. Then music came into the background as I held on.

"Team B, can I help you?" A new voice. "Yes, I would like to make an appointment to see one of your psychiatrists," I answered.

"Your name please." I gave her my name. "Your address," she questioned. I told her. "Your age . . ."

The appointment was set for two o'clock the next afternoon. I hung up wondering if they were going to lock me up and throw away the key. There was nothing that I feared more than that. The threat of two years before had continued to loom over me. And I was convinced that if I made one slip it was off to the slammer with me. The padded room where people beat their heads against the wall. Shock therapy. More medication. Doctors probing into my head. A lobotomy . . .

The next day I slept late, knowing that my only scheduled activity was the trip to the loony bin. "Maybe I shouldn't go," I

convinced myself as I headed to my car. "I can make it without
help." But a voice deep within convinced me differently. "YOU
NEED HELP!!"

But by the time I reached the hospital I had become uncon-
trollably hysterical. The receptionist took one look at me and
quickly asked me to sit on one of the couches. She rang the doctor
on the intercom to let him know my state. Then she handed me a
glass of water and asked me to drink it all.

After what seemed like hours, a doctor walked up to me and introduced himself. "My name is Dr. Austin. Come this way," he
said, as he pointed down the hall. I followed him and sank into a
chair when we got to his office. He closed the door.

"Tell me about yourself," he said, looking at me intently.

I began to recall the events of the past two years. "I always
have this dark cloud of doom over me, and I can't break it. Sometimes I just get so afraid of what will happen and that someone
will hurt me. When I feel like that, I hide in my room until it
passes. And I used to just drop in and out of reality, as I was able
to handle it. Sometimes I still go into this other world and just
rest. I don't have anywhere else to go." I choked.

He listened with great concentration and continued to question
me until he was satisfied that he had learned enough. "I think I
could work with you," he said. "I can see you once a week and
we'll try to sort out all your feelings. It's going to take a long time
for you to get well. I can't promise you instant success. It took
years for you to get sick and it will take some time to make you
well. Would you like to work with me?" he asked.

"Sure," I said. "I don't have much choice." He nodded his head
and set up our first appointment, for the following week. I rose to
leave but remembered one last thing.

"Will you need my files from Dr. Dane, the psychiatrist I told
you about in Willis?" I asked. "He knows everything about me."

"No, that's not necessary," he answered. "I think I have
enough here to work with. You and I have a lot of sorting out to
do."

I said good-bye and walked out of the room. A great sense of relief came over me. I had not told him that I'd been diagnosed as a
paranoid schizophrenic. Purposely, I had left out many details of

my past, not wanting to give him grounds to commit me to the hospital. I knew that I was not half as crazy as I'd been right after my breakdown. God had brought me a long way from that and I didn't want this man to throw my past in my face. I didn't know him and I didn't trust him—yet. He would have to earn the right to know all my secrets. I felt the need to hide just one thing—the fact that I'd been declared "insane." God had told me that He would heal me. And I was forced to believe that. But, there was no way I could explain that to a psychiatrist. If I told him that God talked to me, it would probably give him grounds to put me away. Most schizophrenics have delusions, but no one in the world was going to tell me that God was one of my delusions.

I arrived home in a complete state of mental disarray to find that two of my roommates had moved in. I was so exhausted that all I could say was "Hello" and retreat to my room to pull myself together. I fell asleep and awoke the next day. Debbie had left the previous night and two more girls appeared that morning.

Kelly, the head of the house, sat me down to tell me how she planned on running the house. "We want to make this a tight, close little community. So, we plan on eating together at night, sharing the cleaning duties and cooking. But, most of all, we'll have a house meeting once a week to pray together and share our lives," she said. "We want you to join us," she added.

I looked at her for a moment, wondering what I had gotten into. All I had asked for was a room to call my own. I had not asked for a family. I had had no intention of becoming part of a religious community. But I felt trapped and could see no way out.

As I thought this through, Kelly continued. "We live by faith. That's how God's called us to live. We need to get close so we can all survive," she said. And then she smiled. I tried to force a smile in return.

I walked to my room to think over my predicament. I didn't want to be close to these girls. I had always carefully chosen my friends from among the many people I met. And I felt as though five people had just shoved their lives under my nose, expecting me to be happy that they had done so. I was more afraid of these people than I'd ever been of anyone in my life. I didn't know how to act. I didn't know what to say.

I walked back to the living room and sat down with the other girls. Faith, June, Betty, and Nadine looked excited about living together. Kelly took a piece of paper and divided the housework, scheduled each of us for cooking and dishwashing, and then began to talk about finances.

"We'll each contribute seventy-five dollars a month for rent. Food shouldn't run us more than ten dollars a week. We have to pay for our own heat, and that may run fifty dollars a month, plus utilities. I'll take care of the bills and let you each know when they're due. Is that o.k.?" she asked. Everyone chimed, "Fine!" And the saga began.

The first house meeting was at five in the morning. Kelly woke me, along with the other girls and we met in the living room. Prayer was at the top of the list, as was sharing our problems and concerns. I, however, was still sleepy, and when I closed my eyes to pray I fell off. At the end of the meeting, Kelly woke me and told me what had happened. I got up and walked to my room, climbing into bed to catch a few winks. And so it went every week.

I wanted little to do with the girls I lived with. I had believed that Arlene had shared my problems with them and they knew why I was so depressed, withdrawn, and spaced out. But she hadn't and I had to face that prospect alone.

"Judy, can you hear me?" June asked as she touched my hand. "I've been speaking to you and you're just staring into space."

I looked at her for a moment, wondering how to explain the blackouts I had. "I'm sorry," I answered. "Sometimes I just slip out of reality. I can't help it," I pleaded, looking into her eyes for understanding.

"Do you want to talk about it?" she asked. I studied her face and saw that she was concerned and interested. I started to tell her my story and sat for many hours explaining all the things that had happened to me.

"I'm trying to find some answer to my problems," I explained. "But, there don't seem to be any. . . ."

"Well, trust God and he'll make it better," she added. "He has a way of doing things like that."

I looked at her, anger rising inside. "I *have*," I said. "And He *doesn't do anything*: Don't give me your religious garbage. I've heard enough of that to make me sick. God doesn't just zap away your problems. I *know that for a fact*. So, just leave me alone, o.k.?" I yelled.

June stepped away, hurt by what I had said. I was sure she was thinking that I didn't have enough faith. And I had been told that five hundred times in the past. "If you believe," the Christians I'd known had told me, "then God will do the rest." If only it were that easy!

June got up and walked out of the room. I determined in my heart to shut the girls out of my life and go my own way. I didn't need their religious pressure.

On Sundays all the girls would go to church together. At first, I went with them, to a born-again Methodist church down the street. I wanted to see who went there and what it was like. But for me it was no different from any other church I'd been to. It offered me nothing. So I stopped going.

This, along with the fact that I did not keep up my end of the housecleaning, angered my roommates. They noticed that I wanted very little to do with them and cared even less what happened in the house. I had shut myself off in a way that angered them. To top it all off, they noticed that I often skipped days of classes at secretarial school. And they felt they had to do something about it.

For a time, they had let it pass. But one evening I walked into the house and the crew was sitting in the living room waiting for me. I knew by the looks on their faces that they didn't plan on throwing bouquets of roses at my feet. I tried to duck into my room to escape the ordeal ahead, but was pulled into the living room.

"We don't like the way you've been acting," Kelly said, her hands on her hips. "You don't seem to care about anyone but yourself. You don't do your cleaning around here, you take off on Friday when it's your turn to cook. Besides that, you act nasty and selfish. I think it stinks," she added.

"Yeah," Faith piped in. "You are very selfish. And you don't know how to love. Don't you think it's pretty crazy to be seeing a non-Christian therapist? He can't help you. Only God can. You shouldn't see him."

"You don't even try," Betty added. "We're your friends and we want to help you. . . ." Their voices all came at me and I wanted to scream.

"If you want to help me, then why don't you leave me alone? I never asked you to be my friends. I never asked you to care. What right do you have to judge and condemn me? None of you are any better than I am. You just look better on the outside. You don't know what goes on inside my head, or my heart. And I think you're all pretty rotten. You have no right to tell me how to live. . . ." I screamed as I ran to my room.

I pulled the pillow over my head and began to cry. I had seen, for the first time in a while, something that I had always believed. Christians were no different than anyone else. Just because they had Christ in their lives was no guarantee that they would be loving, kind, or understanding. They just believed that they were. I got more understanding from the non-Christians I knew. And I preferred to spend time with them than to listen to pious verbosity. Religious people, it seemed to me, always had a way to prove everyone but themselves wrong. And the guilt I felt was killing me. I would never be good enough for God or anyone else. No matter how hard I tried, it was never good enough. I was a failure.

I had an appointment with my psychiatrist the next afternoon and stayed in bed until an hour before. I hadn't been to classes in three days and was behind in my shorthand. I knew that I should get up and work on it, but I just didn't care. There was no reason to work at anything since I failed in everything I did. Life again looked hopeless. And I believed that God had deserted me. I hadn't heard from Him in months.

I made my way into the psychiatrist's office in a state of deep depression. Seeing him also seemed useless. We had made no progress and had solved no problems. I sat down, thinking that maybe I should just sign myself into the hospital and quit pretending that I could sort out my life. The idea looked better than what I was dealing with in the present. I had no strength to go on, and I didn't even care anymore what became of me. "Don't kid yourself," I thought. "You're never getting better. Stop believing that you will."

Dr. Austin began to speak and I tried to concentrate on what he was saying. "Judy, I've been transferred to another section of the hospital. I won't be able to see you anymore," he said.

"So, tell me what I should do," I answered. "Where do I go from here?" I was hoping he'd say I was going to be admitted into the hospital.

"I have a friend here who I think could help you. His name is Paul. I want you to meet him," he said. Then he picked up the intercom and called him. I sat in my chair, my heart pounding with fear of meeting another person. "I'm not ready," I thought, as Paul walked in the room.

Dr. Austin introduced us and then left the room. "You should take this time to get to know one another. I'll be outside."

"Tell me something about yourself," Paul asked. Belligerently, I looked at him, wondering how to approach this new guy. I wanted to push him as far away from me as possible.

"I'm a paranoid schizophrenic," I said. "That means that I'm not in touch with reality. I can't think or concentrate. And I'm afraid of people. But, mostly I'm a failure. I have failed at everything I've ever done. If anything in life is going to go wrong it finds me and goes wrong in my lap."

"Did you always feel this way?" he asked.

"Only since I was about thirteen," I said. "Before that I was a good person. But, I went rotten in my thirteenth year. They tell me there's no hope for me. Why do you bother trying to help?" I asked.

"Do you really believe that you're a bad person?" he asked. "I don't think anyone is completely bad. And I don't think anyone is a complete failure. Don't you think you're a little hard on yourself?" he asked.

"No," I answered. "If I don't get hard on me, who will? Who will keep me in line?"

"How long have you been so overweight?" he asked. I looked at my body and tried to cover it.

"Well, I was at my normal weight when I first went to college. Maybe five pounds over. But I looked good. When I got on all that medicine, I started gaining weight and haven't stopped," I said.

"What size do you wear?" he asked.

Shocked at his frankness, I was afraid not to answer. "Twenty," I said.

"So why don't you lose some weight?" he asked.

Shocked again, I answered, "I don't know. I've tried but I can't seem to do it."

"I think you're afraid to trust anyone," he said to me. "You're afraid of taking the risk of love and losing again. And that's why you're paranoid and scared. That's why you're not close to anyone. And that's why you have stayed overweight. You don't want anyone to get near you—least of all a man," he said. "Am I right?"

"I don't know," I answered. "I've never thought about it before. Who are you to ask all these personal questions? You don't act like a psychiatrist."

"I'm not a psychiatrist. I only have my bachelor's degree in psychology. But, I know what it's like to struggle and I think I can help you."

"But I was told that there was little I could do besides learn to live with my illness," I said.

"Judy," he said, "did you take a good look at this hospital when you came in? It's huge and it's full of people with diagnoses much the same as yours. Some of them have been in institutions most of their lives. And they have learned how to maintain their sickness. They get so involved in their illness that they don't try to deal with some of their current problems. They mull over the past and live in guilt all their lives.

"From talking to you," he went on, "I can see that you've come a long way since your breakdown. I don't claim to know how to make you well. All that I can do is help you look at yourself today and give you the encouragement to start some change in your life. By seeing and talking with you today, I know that there are several areas where you can begin. You have a rotten self-image. You're scared to death of people. You hate yourself. You hate the world. You don't think anyone loves you. You're extremely overweight. Don't you realize that the combination of all those things is enough to drive anyone insane? And to top it all off, you are convinced that there is no way out. You live in a cloud of doom. And if I had to deal with all that, day in and day out, I would probably retreat into a fantasy world myself. You have good reason to have gone over the deep end. But, you have no reason to stay there forever."

I looked at him as he continued.

"People deal with their problems in many ways. Some people, given your circumstances might become so embittered that they would kill. Less sensitive folks would have let much of it pass right over them and wouldn't have taken to heart the things that you have. Someone of a different temperament might have compensated by excelling in a career. You, however, because of your makeup, became a schizophrenic. But, that does not mean that you can't begin to work out your problems. Your problems are obvious and I think this is the time in your life to start working on them," he said.

"I did a lot of LSD," I said. "And I still feel the effect of it. I can't walk into a crowded room without feeling smothered. I can't stand bright lights or loud noise. There's so much distortion in my mind. I can't even think straight," I added.

"But you can learn to think again. You don't know for sure what influence the drugs had on your mind. You're so overwhelmed by so many bad feelings and so much confusion that you can't see the forest for the trees. But, there's only one place to begin. And that's to take one problem at a time, breaking it down, sorting it out. Talking it over. I think that will start a healing process in your life."

"But, you don't know that for sure," I said. "You're not even a psychiatrist."

"You're right," he said. "I'm not. I don't have a lot of degrees. I don't have any fancy titles. And I reject traditional psychotherapy. I'm a Reality Therapist."

"What's that?" I asked.

"Well, in a nutshell, Reality Therapy says that a person is responsible for who they are. They can't blame it on the past, or people in the past. You have to take responsibility for who you are today and correct the things that are wrong in the present. I don't think that mulling over the past cures anyone. Sometimes you have to talk about the past to understand who you are today, but you can't live there. I think that if you work on your present problems you'll come out of this all right, Judy," he said.

"Well, I've never heard of this before," I said. "I don't know if it will work for me."

"So, look at it this way," he said. "It's your last option. My time is up, but I'd like to see you on Monday, Wednesday, and Friday at noon. Can you make it?" he asked.

"Sure," I said, as I stood and walked to the door. "See you then."

Paul stopped me at the door and looked me straight in the eyes. "In the meantime, think about why you hate yourself so much. We'll work on that first," he added.

I walked out the door and got into my car. Sitting for a moment, I closed my eyes and began to pray. Before I could say much, God interrupted me.

"That man is right," He said. "And he's the one I'm going to use to heal you."

"But what about the damage the LSD has done to my mind?" I asked. "Talking about it won't heal me," I said.

"You do your part," God said to me. "And I will heal your mind."

"I think it's all rather crazy," I said to God. "But, I like Paul 'cause he talks straight to me. He doesn't treat me like I'll break."

"He has no intention of breaking you," God said. "Like me, he wants to see you get well."

10   And the Truth Shall Set You Free

I drove home thinking over Paul's question. "Do I really hate myself?" I asked. "Or is it that other people hate me?" I pulled into the driveway, wondering which it was.

I remembered that my mother was coming for the weekend. And I couldn't figure out why she always came at the wrong time. She had a way of showing up when I least wanted to see her.

I was in no mood to listen to her physical complaints. She had been ill for many years, with one thing or another. Everytime I talked to her, it was something new. Just recently she had been in the hospital and called to ask me if she could come "rest" for a while at my place. There was no way I could say no.

So, I agreed to let her come. I was thankful, however, that I was working and would be gone most of the time. It would make things much easier for me.

I had completed secretarial school two weeks before. The placement office had arranged an interview for me with one of the local papers. They had hired me and I started work the next day. It was my first full-time job—a place where I had to be every day. And I was trying to take it seriously. The pay stank, but it kept me busy and got me off welfare. I was thankful for that.

My mother arrived the next day and I immediately went into an emotional panic. The years between us had created a distance that I was content not to bridge—not *now!!* I felt no closeness to her and didn't even feel as though she were my mother. And I didn't know how to be her daughter. There was no "going back."

I tried to be kind to her and to listen when I had time. But I felt nothing for her, no love, no sympathy, no compassion. My heart was dead. She slept on the couch and since she had been very ill, she was unable to move around much. I gave her my TV set and she entertained herself by watching it all day and night.

The time of her visit passed quickly. I was thankful for that, because there were battles raging within me which I felt deserved priority. The morning she left, I felt as though a two-hundred-pound weight had been taken off my shoulders. I could relax again.

My roommates had watched, during those days, my interaction with my mother. And the day she left, they called me in for a "conference," saying they wanted to talk to me about her visit. I knew by the looks on their faces that I was in for trouble, but I sat down to hear them out.

"You are a very unloving person," Faith said to me. "While your mother was here, you hardly spent any time with her at all. You weren't even nice to her sometimes. I don't think you act like a Christian at all. How can you call yourself a Christian and act the way you did?" she asked.

"I doubt that you've really been saved," Nadine added. "If you were really saved, you would have love in your heart for people. But you just don't have it," she added.

The conversation continued, as each roommate gave her opinion of my spiritual life. I stared at them as they babbled on. My mind was blown by their comments and judgments—and I couldn't find words to answer for myself. I headed to my room in tears.

"Don't you have anything to say for yourself?" Nadine asked. I looked back at her, searching for a rebuttal. But there was nothing inside me with which I could answer. "I guess that God will have to prove all of you wrong. I am born again, I just have some problems that aren't worked out yet," I said. "I don't know how to deal with people like you."

I ran into my bedroom and flung myself on my bed and buried

my face in my pillow. I wondered how people could be so cruel—Christians at that—but I could come up with no answer. I turned on my TV and waited for the time to pass until I could leave for my counseling appointment with Paul.

I drove to his office thinking that maybe life was just too hard for me to handle after all. I wanted to give up. No one was helping me piece my life together and I was discouraged enough to throw in the towel and admit defeat.

"Have you thought about my question?" Paul asked, as I walked through his door.

I started to speak but broke into tears. "What happened to you?" he asked. "What upset you so badly?"

I started to tell him about my meeting with my roommates that morning. I was crying so hard that I felt as though I was going to throw up. Slowly, as I poured out my complaint, I began to feel better and could calm myself down.

"How can I like myself!?" I yelled at him. "No one else likes me. I have a mother who constantly reminds me of what a lousy daughter I am. I have roommates who tell me that I don't know how to love. No matter what I do, it's not good enough. I'm never perfect enough. *Never.* People want to change me because I'm bad the way I am," I cried.

"Judy," Paul said. "Did you feel like your parents loved you when you were a child?" he asked.

"They didn't love me," I yelled. "They were always too busy working, drinking, or fighting to have time for me. I was just an afterthought. A problem to them. When I was down, no one ever tried to help me. They told me that the way I felt was stupid. I wasn't allowed to really feel bad about something. I had to be strong. And when I wasn't, they told me I was stupid," I cried.

"Do you believe that?" he asked. "Do you think you are stupid?"

I sat for a moment, pondering his question. "Yeah, I am stupid. I must be. If I wasn't, people would love me. They would understand. Everything I've ever done was wrong or stupid. I never did anything right. Look at my breakdown. Now, that was really stupid," I said.

"But do you think they hated you?" Paul asked.

"Yeah, they hated me. They didn't care about me. All they cared about was themselves," I answered.

"You mean they didn't care about how you felt?" he asked.

"I guess so," I said, my temper rising. "There were times when I needed help and encouragement." I began to tell him about the time when my father remarried, the time my mother had left. The time when I had my breakdown. "They weren't there to help me," I continued. "I was alone. I've always been alone. I never knew how to help myself. I didn't know how to change. No one helped me—no one even cared. They were too busy," I cried.

"Do you think that maybe they didn't understand? I don't think that people hurt us intentionally," he said.

"Well, I do," I answered. "They knew what they were doing. They knew that they could hurt me by not trying to help me."

"Sometimes people just don't know how to help," Paul continued. "And some people are afraid of their emotions. You were displaying a lot of negative emotions during those times. It must have frightened them horribly. They didn't know how to deal with it, so they pushed it away from them. And in doing that, they pushed you away," he said.

"Well, that's wonderful," I said. "I've always been on my own. I can't make it on my own. I need help. And no one will ever help me."

"Do you think that maybe they didn't like themselves? People who don't like themselves find it hard to love others. Maybe they had problems of their own and couldn't handle yours on top of theirs. And sometimes people want us to live up to their expectations. It sounds like they wanted you to be a certain way—to live up to their standards. And that's impossible for anyone to do," he added.

I looked up at him. I had never heard anyone talk like this. Why was he defending them? How could he believe that they weren't just rotten people. He made them sound good.

"Did your father ever do anything for you?" Paul questioned. I thought for a moment before answering.

"Well, he used to give me money. He gave me money to use for expenses at college."

"So that's one way of showing love," he said. "Some people

only know how to show love by giving another person a present."

"I didn't want his presents," I answered. "I wanted him to hold me and tell me that everything would be o.k. That would have been enough."

"You know, Judy, you react so negatively to people because you expect far too much of them. You have to learn that you are not the only one who has weaknesses, or flaws. Your father was trying. You don't have the corner on suffering. Other people feel pain, and in expecting these people to be perfect, you will always be disappointed. Not only must you accept yourself the way you are, but you must accept others the way they are.

"Well, think about this and we'll talk about it again." He stood up to let me out of the door. I wished I didn't have to leave.

I walked out of his office humiliated, yet knowing that God had spoken to me through Paul. It was the hardest, of all the things I was learning, to accept. And yet I knew, at that moment, that his words were a key to my healing.

I drove to work, my face swollen from crying. I was in no mood to talk to anyone and I hoped the day would go smoothly. I walked to my desk and sat down. A pile of copy was waiting for me.

My job was sometimes very exciting to me. All my life I had wanted to be a writer and now I was working with newswriters and editors. I worked on the copy desk, typing copy for the computer, setting computer codes, and proofreading what I had done. Most days I typed straight for eight hours, but I didn't mind. There was so much to learn.

I studied all that was put in front of me. I started to learn the style of the paper and could catch mistakes that the editors missed. I also became knowledgeable in computer typesetting. I could set almost anything for type.

My boss, Frank Harvey, was very pleased with my work. He sensed that I learned quickly and gave me extra jobs to do. Often, he would sit with me for an hour or two and teach me how to edit copy and write headlines.

"You'll be a copy editor by the end of this year," he said to me as he described type sizes to me. "You're sharper than most the people I have on my desk. I could use you," he said. He gave me some headlines to study. "You have to say it all in one line and catch the reader's attention," he added. Then he pulled out an AP Style Book. "Study this and learn everything in it. When the time is right, I'm having you promoted. It won't be for a while, so take your time. Learn it right."

No one had ever taken time with me, to teach me or care about the work I was doing. Working at my job built confidence in my talents. I felt as though I had a future and I knew I could do well for myself.

Often, after work, I would stop at Ann's house for a few hours. I liked being around her because we had old times to talk about and she made me feel comfortable. She had no gripes with me about how I lived or what I believed. She just liked me the way I was. At that time of my life, I needed that acceptance more than I needed anything else in the world.

But, I began to feel uneasy about going to her house. She, her boy friend, and their friends were dealing heavily in drugs and I thought that they would probably get busted. I knew I shouldn't put my life on the line, but I wanted to be around her. So, I continued the association. And I usually saw her on Friday, my night off.

"Ann, you want to go out for a while?" I asked. "There's a good movie playing on campus."

"No, we're expecting friends tonight. I have to be here. Why don't you come over and meet them?" she asked.

"O.k.," I said. "I'll be over around eight o'clock."

At seven-thirty I jumped into my car and tried to start it. But the engine would not turn over. I walked around to the back and opened the hood. Fiddling with the wires, I hoped I could get it to go. But the car wouldn't cooperate. I tried again and again, but the engine was dead.

I became angry. "You do nothing but cost me money," I said to the car. "More bills. You think money grows on trees. I can't afford you." I climbed out and kicked the wheel. "Get well," I said, as I headed to the house. "I can't afford a sick car."

I walked inside and into my room. Turning on the TV, I waited for time to pass so I could try it again. At nine o'clock, I went outside and turned the key. The engine was still dead.

Giving up and very frustrated, I walked back inside. Picking up the phone, I dialed Ann's number and waited for her to answer. But the phone kept ringing and no one picked up. "That's really weird," I said to myself. "This just isn't my night." So, I retired to my room and turned on the TV again.

At eleven o'clock the news came on. I wasn't paying much attention, my mind wandering through other things. But suddenly it caught my attention.

"The Andor Police Department reports they have made the biggest drug bust in the history of this city. Two men and one woman were arrested on the south side at eight-thirty this evening. Police confiscated two pounds of marijuana, narcotic paraphernalia. . . ."

My eyes almost dropped out of their sockets. I squinted to watch the newsreel and saw Ann's house in the background. My heart fell to my stomach.

I grabbed my car keys and ran outside. I put the key in and turned. AND THE CAR STARTED!! I couldn't believe it! God had stopped me from going to Ann's and being busted with her. I didn't know He could do such things.

I tried to reach Ann the next day. But she wasn't out of jail. Finally, I turned her over to God and waited for her call. I prayed that God would be with her and that He would use this as an opportunity to bring her to Him. I found out later that she had never given Him a second thought. "I can take care of myself," she said when she called. "I don't need God."

The following week, I received a call from Buddy. I had been so busy worrying about Ann that I'd forgotten to call her.

"Judy, I have to talk to you," Buddy said. "Do you have some time?"

"Sure," I answered. "I always have time for you. Do you want to come over?" I asked.

"Yeah," she said. "I'll grab a bus and be there in about an hour."

I sat waiting for her to arrive. I couldn't figure out what was wrong. Finally the door bell rang and I let Buddy in. Pointing to my room, we walked inside and closed the door.

"Judy, I was riding past a church the other day and God told me that he wanted me to accept Jesus—like you have. It was so real to me, but I don't know how to do it. What do I do?" she asked.

"Bow your head," I said. "And pray after me." I prayed the sinner's prayer and she prayed after me. When we finished, Buddy threw her arms around me and hugged me. Her eyes were full of joy. She was the last person in the world I'd expected to be converted. I couldn't believe that God had used me to save a soul. My spirits and confidence were lifted.

My times with Paul were getting better. I could be open and honest with him about all the things I felt inside. Sharing my pain and anger became a less frightening thing. And I began to realize that what I felt was very common and not weird at all. Up to this point I had believed that my emotions were "sick" and bad. I had tried to repress them, hoping they'd go away. Now that I had the freedom to let them out, my depression lessened, and I was learning that I was a fragile, precious human being. And I found that very delightful.

"You're looking better," Paul said to me as I walked in his office. "You're starting to feel better about yourself, aren't you?"

"Well, I've thought a lot about my parents and it hit me the other day that they really did love me. I guess I'm more able to see them as people instead of infallible gods. It was hard to see for a long time, but I think they did love me," I said.

"That must make you feel better about yourself," Paul said. "Once you learn that you are lovable, people don't seem so frightening. How are you doing with your present relationships?"

"Well, I'm still a little afraid of people. I don't want to be rejected, I guess."

"We're all afraid of rejection," Paul said. "That's why we run away from intimacy and closeness. To avoid the potential hurt in a relationship. Love is a risk. And when you love someone you take the risk of being hurt," he added.

"I haven't really reached out to anyone in the past few years. I don't know how to handle relationships. I don't know what to say or how to act. It doesn't come naturally with me. I just feel awkward," I said.

"But you've had a lot of problems this year—and in years past. You have a lot of legitimate rejection behind you. Maybe it's time you stepped past that. Somewhere along the line you'll have to reach out again," he said.

"Yeah," I said. "I'm just afraid people will want to remake me. And so often I set myself up with people like that. I try to be myself, but it's easier to be what someone wants you to be. It's kind of like buying their love."

"You're going through a lot of struggle right now. Finding yourself is not easy. You often learn by making mistakes. But you shouldn't let people walk on you just because you're weak. And you shouldn't avoid people just because you're unsure of yourself. You'll gain confidence by trying again," he said.

"Why do I always have to meet people where they're at? I never seem to find a friend, except Buddy, who just likes me the way I am. She likes to do what I like to do. My Christian friends like to go to Bible studies and prayer meetings. There have to be other things to do, other ways to spend time with Christians.

"Have you ever asked any of your Christian friends to do something with you that you like to do?" he asked.

"No, I didn't think there was much hope that anyone would want to do what I want. I didn't see much hope for my relationships with my roommates," I added. I sat for a moment, thinking about what I had said.

"Paul," I said. "It's so hard for me to love myself. And I think that it must be that hard for other people. I see all my weak areas and I wonder how anyone could love that."

"I think you expect too much of yourself," he said. "You have to accept yourself as having weak areas. And when you accept that, you will love those parts of yourself and stop looking for love from other people. At that point, you'll be free," he added.

I sat pondering his statements. "Is that true?" I asked. "Is it only a matter of self-acceptance?"

"In your case it is. When you like yourself and accept yourself, Judy, you aren't so hard on yourself for your mistakes. You are a perfectionist and you have many illusions about yourself and other people. But they aren't realistic. They are dreams. You need to think about them and weed out the illusions. You do have the ability to deal with reality. You just don't think that you do. Your sickness was a way of running away from reality because you didn't know how to deal with it. But I think you can handle it now. You have no choice," he said.

"Are you trying to help me love myself?" I asked. "You always see the good things in me and remind me of them. And you also see the good in the people I talk about. Is life really a matter of acceptance and love?"

"It's all *you* need," he said. "Ninety per cent of your problems are based in a lack of self-acceptance. You will be well when you learn to love yourself," he continued.

"Wow," I said. "You make it sound so easy."

"It's simple," he said, "but it's not easy. It takes time and work." I wondered if God accepted me the way I was. In my mind I had always believed that. But in my heart, I was not sure.

Lying in bed that evening, I thought about that subject again. "How do I learn to love myself?" I wondered. "If I could do that, ninety per cent of my problems would be gone."

Reading and thinking, I mulled over the thought. As I lay in bed, a warm peace came over me. The room filled with light and I knew that Jesus was standing in the room with me. Slowly, His words crept into my heart.

"I love you the way you are," Jesus said to me. "I don't want you to be someone else. I made you the way you are and when you stop fighting my creation you will be free."

As He spoke, a warmth and peace filled my body and mind. I began to cry, tears that had been hidden deep inside me for many years. Many of my emotional walls—protective barriers—began to break. I knew that Jesus had done a deep healing in my heart.

I returned to Paul's office, a new person. The depression that had loomed over me for years was broken. My spirit and my heart were light. My head no longer spun from thought to thought. Paul was pleased at this change and breakthrough in my life.

I was out of medication and asked him to refill my prescription. "You don't need that stuff," he said to me. "You are now strong enough to make it on your own. Try to do without it."

I rode home, angry at him for cutting me off. What right did he have to make that judgment for me? I was steaming as I walked into my room and turned on my stereo. There was no way

I could make it without the medicine. Hadn't Dr. Dane told me that I would need it for the rest of my life?

As I listened to the music, my heart softened and a small voice within began to speak. "Take what you have left and flush it down the toilet. You don't need to take it anymore. You are free from your medication."

The words came at me with such conviction that I was sure it was God's voice. Obediently, I took my jars of pills and flushed them all down the toilet.

During my first two drug-free days I felt better than I had in years. The sleepiness I felt went away. My mind cleared and so did my eyes. My senses were sharper and I began to feel things I hadn't felt in a long time. At first it was a nice change, but after a while the emotions I felt overwhelmed me. I could feel the slightest mood change. I could feel anger, frustration, pain, and love. I had not experienced such intense emotions in quite some time.

Frightened by what was happening to me, my body began to shake. I kept thinking that I wasn't going to make it without the pills. In panic, I paced the floor, crying, screaming at myself in my room. And I refused to go to work.

Kelly saw how upset I was and suggested that I go with her to visit an evangelist who was in the area. "She could pray over you," Kelly said. "Maybe that would help." But, before we left, I called Dr. Dane in Willis and asked him why I was having so much trouble.

"Judy, you aren't supposed to go cold turkey. You should have slowly decreased your dosage. Your body is going through shock. It's no wonder you feel terrible," he said.

I felt like a junkie coming off heroin. I was scared and believed that I wasn't going to pull through. I pictured my body going through convulsions and then giving up in defeat. I was hooked, psychologically addicted to the drugs. These thoughts in mind, I drove with Kelly to visit the evangelist.

When we arrived, she asked me what was wrong and I explained about the drugs. Laying hands on me, she began to pray. "Jesus, I ask you to free this girl from these drugs. Give her the faith to let go. Give her the strength to keep fighting. And bind Satan from her mind and heart. Thank you, Jesus."

I looked up at her when she had finished. "You must steep yourself in the Scriptures. Satan is going to do anything he can to convince you that you can't make it. You're fighting a spiritual battle and God wants you to win. Don't give up, Judy. Fight with all that you have. And pray for faith," she added.

I thanked her for her prayers and left. I didn't feel any different. My body was still shaking, my mind reeling. And deep in my heart I didn't believe that I would make it. I drove to work and kept repeating Scripture to myself. "I can do all things through Christ who strengthens me," I said. "Greater is He who is in you than he who is in the world." Over and over again I repeated those verses. Several days went like that.

But one morning I woke up and my head was clear. I waited for the assaulting thoughts, but they did not come. Sitting on my bed, I listened to the silence. My mind and body were at rest. My heart was filled with peace. Suddenly, I jumped up and started dancing around the room.

"I made it, Jesus. I really made it. I'm free. I'm healed," I yelled. I hugged myself and cried. And cried. My joy was overflowing, the thrill of victory seeping into every part of my being. I would never be sick again. I could start to live a normal life.

My next appointment with Paul was the best I'd ever had. I felt, for the first time in my life, that I was emotionally free. I felt strong.

I could love myself and I could love others. Paul and I talked about my future—where I'd go from there. I wanted to return to college to get my degree in journalism and become a writer. But Paul had different ideas.

"You're still weak," he said. "You've come a long way, but give yourself some time to build strength. Don't rush out to conquer the world. It's just not ready for you."

"Oh, don't be so pessimistic," I said. "I worked hard for the victory. Don't take it away from me. I can make it now. I'm going to apply for college. I'm going to finish my degree. Nothing can stop me now."

"Well," Paul said, "take it slow and think over your decisions.

Don't rush into anything. You're on a high right now. Don't let it fool you. You still have a lot of room for growth."

"O.k., you old fuddy-duddy," I said. "Even if you don't believe in me, I do."

I rode home that afternoon feeling as though I had slain a dragon. I didn't think there was anything I couldn't do—a complete change from four months earlier. My depression was gone, the grievous pain I had felt for years was cleansed from my system and I was free of drugs. It was exciting to be this new person.

But, there were many loose ends in my life—things that God wanted to work out for me. The most pressing issue was my relationships with my roommates. We had reached a stalemate and neither side was giving in. The tension wore on all of us and God decided to put an end to it.

Kelly had been visiting Arlene one day, complaining about the way I acted toward her and the problems she felt I brought upon the household. She had expected that Arlene would side with her, but God had turned the tables.

"You know," Arlene said to Kelly, "when Judy comes here and talks about you girls, I always defend you. And now I must defend her. I don't think that you really believe in her. You think that she is a failure and you treat her that way. But Jesus Christ lives within her. And for that reason, He is going to hold her up and put her life together. You have no right to judge God's work in her life, her progress, or spiritual condition. You have not been Christ-like in your behavior toward her. Your attitude is a stench before God," she said. "I think that you and all the girls owe Judy an apology."

Kelly stood, staring at Arlene. "Do you really think she is trying?" she asked. "It sure doesn't look like it right now."

"The trouble is that you girls do not see her as Christ sees her. And He sees her as perfect, the way she is. She is right where God wants her right now and you have no right to tell her differently. You judge by appearance. God judges the heart. And you don't know what is in her heart," she said.

After that conversation, Kelly came running home, convinced of her own guilt. She shared with the girls what Arlene had said and when I walked in the house that afternoon, they were sitting in the living room waiting for me. They asked me to come sit with them because they wanted to talk. I was reluctant to go another round with them, but something inside me told me not to say no. I walked into the living room and sat down.

"Judy," Kelly said, "I want to ask you to forgive me for the way I've acted toward you. I haven't been accepting you the way you are and I know that's wrong."

"Me, too," Nadine said. "You have been honest with us about where you're at and we just couldn't accept that. I guess we haven't been very honest with you. Just mean. Will you forgive me?"

I sat listening, as each girl took her turn to ask my forgiveness. It was the first time in my life that I had been absolved of guilt in a relationship. No one had ever come back and told me that I was right.

"Of course I forgive you," I said, looking each girl in the eye. "Can you forgive me? I haven't really tried to see things as you see them. I don't really understand your way of looking at life. I haven't kept up my end of the housework and I can be pretty nasty sometimes."

We all stood and hugged one another, breaking the tension that had been between us for several months. We had finally become that community Kelly had talked about when I first moved in. But it had come about in God's way and in His time. And also, under His conditions.

With this behind me, a greater sense of confidence and faith began to build in my life. I knew that it was time to "take a risk" as Paul had talked about. It was time to reach out to someone whom I wanted to be friends with.

I met Katy at a wedding, early that spring. All year I had wanted to get to know her but hadn't had the guts to reach out to her. And God had arranged it so she sat right across from me at the wedding. We had a chance to warm up to each other and begin a friendship.

The following Monday, I called her and asked her if she wanted to have lunch with me. She was excited to say "yes" and I drove to her office at noon. Waiting for me at the door, she grabbed her coat and we walked across the street to a small restaurant.

"You know, Judy, I have heard your roommates talk about you all year. And I don't think you're at all the way they described you. I was expecting some kind of monster or freak. I don't find you selfish or unloving," she said.

"Well, you should have known me six months ago," I said, as I recalled all the growth I had experienced. "I've grown up a lot this year and I've learned to love myself. It's hard to like people when you don't like yourself. It took me a long time to find out that I was lovable."

"You must be very special to Jesus," she said. "He's brought you through a lot of heavy things and He's healed you. Your life is a miracle."

"Yeah, but I was a real weirdo. You didn't know me when I was crazy," I added.

"But, there's no evidence of that now. You're one of the most stable people I've ever met. And the most honest."

"Do you mean that?" I asked. "I like myself now. I think I became crazy because I couldn't be honest—or realistic. I lived in an imaginary world that was filled with pain. I don't need that anymore."

"I don't see why you wouldn't be lovable," she said. "You're easy to be with. You make me feel comfortable. I just know that I could tell you anything. You wouldn't be shocked, would you?" she asked.

"After what I've been through, nothing could shock me. I've seen the worst of life," I said.

"God is really going to bless you," she answered. "You obeyed Him. You stepped out in faith and He made you well. I think that's what Christianity is all about—taking risks and trusting God for the rest."

"Sometimes you don't have a choice," I said. "When things get really bad and everything else fails you—there's only one way to go. And that's up."

Katy smiled at me and stretched her hand across the table. She took my hand in hers, and tears came to her eyes as she spoke. "I really love you, Judy. I don't know you that well, but you are a joy to listen to. You make me realize that our God is very big. Sometimes I need to be reminded of that. Thank you."

I looked back at her. And I smiled. No one had ever called me a joy before. I wasn't sure what it meant, but I knew that it was good.

I drove home that afternoon, knowing that I had made it through the Valley of the Shadow of Death. It had not been by my own strength. It had been by faith, day by day. I recalled the many times I had fallen on my face and wanted to give up. Nothing would ever be that bad again.

I knew that it was time for me to take my place in life.

11 "What Will I Be?"

Taking my place in life meant, first of all, moving into Arlene's house for the summer. She and her husband, Gary, were going to Colorado for staff training and they needed someone to look after their property. I was chosen, along with Susan and Jane, two other girls I knew.

Susan was already living at the house when I moved in. She had been staying with Arlene and Gary for the past six months. Jane had been temporarily staying with the girls I'd lived with that year. So, when I moved, I helped her move her things also.

I walked into Arlene's house with a sigh of relief. I was free from the reminders of the past year's tension. I was on my own. Walking around, I looked over the house and tried to picture it as home in my mind. And it wasn't hard. The place had a warmth and peace about it.

Susan was extremely easy to get along with. Her sense of humor eased my tension. She had a delightful way of looking at life and finding the funny things in it.

But Jane was very different from Susan. She had been a "flower child"—a product of the sixties and early seventies. Her manner was easygoing and her favorite word was "mellow." Her philosophy was that each person should live his life the way he saw fit—and everyone else should keep their hands off it.

But Susan was a very opinionated person. She had grown up in a family with tremendous problems and had developed a definite sense of what was right and wrong. The clash between her and Jane started when she began to push her ideas on Jane.

I tried my best to stay out of the war. I could see both their sides and tended to agree more with Jane. What she was doing was between herself and God and I didn't believe that beating her over the head with values was going to change her. She needed to be accepted the way she was before she would be able to change. But, Susan was of the opinion that it was "her duty" to set Jane straight. Sometimes I thought that God must have a lot of patience to put up with their fighting and not strike them both down for their attitudes. But I prayed for them and kept my mouth shut.

I wanted, most of all, to find out what God wanted me to do with the rest of my life, and then get on with it. I had applied to several state colleges, hoping at least one of them would have an opening for me—and a scholarship. I planned to study journalism, at the suggestion of Mr. Harvey, my boss. He continually encouraged me to become a writer or an editor—whichever I desired most.

But deep inside, I feared success more than I feared failure. I had failed enough in life to know what that was like. Failure was a pretty easy thing to come by—you put out half an effort and when things go wrong you scream, "I can't do it." But success was another story. It meant work.

As I began to think about what I would have to do to become a successful writer or editor, I became very afraid. It was not easy for me to picture myself as a successful person—according to worldly standards. It meant letting go of many of my hangups about myself and stepping out into unknown territory. Working in the business world. Rubbing elbows with people who had "made it." And deep inside me a part of me was screaming, "I can't do it."

All summer I argued with myself about whether or not I really wanted to do something with my life. I was comfortable where I was. I had a job that would eventually turn into a full-time editorial position. I had friends I could depend on. My life was in order (for the first time) and I was afraid to upset that order. I didn't know if I could maintain it under any other circumstances.

But, I also had a sense of restlessness. I knew that if I didn't step out in faith, I'd never know what I was capable of doing. And maybe that would be a source of regrets for the rest of my life. The thought of living with "If Onlys" for the rest of my days did not seem appealing.

For many weeks, I mulled over the many mixed feelings and thoughts within. The price of stepping out seemed too large to handle. It meant possible success. It meant years of working at something until I became good enough to be called a professional. It meant starting at the bottom and working my way up. Most of all, it meant sacrifice. And I had never sacrificed for anything. I had done only what was necessary to survive, avoiding the pain of change at all cost.

All this while, I could not discern what God wanted me to do. Did God want me to step out? Did He want me to follow my desires? Did He want me to trust my intuition? All these things were telling me that it was time to leave. And another part of me was telling me to stay put.

Never in my life had I really thought through a decision. Most of my actions had been rash and impulsive. Counting the cost was not one of my strong points, although this kind of living had always cost me something. I did not trust my judgment as I wished I could. But, I knew that no one else could do it for me. There was nothing to do but trust God to stop me if I was wrong.

So, against all the protests within, I decided to take my giant leap of faith. When I received an acceptance at Hillcrest University, I set my mind on going and finishing my degree. But, it was the hardest and most painful decision I'd ever made. The worst times of my life had been spent in college and the memories returned to overwhelm me when I arrived. I knew that they were only old feelings of days gone by, but it was difficult to get past them. They were real to me—as if they had only happened yesterday. And that was not easy to forget.

I reminded myself that it was not the fault of the college that I had gone crazy. There were many situations there that had helped bring it about. But it was rooted in experiences of a lifetime. I pushed the worries from my mind and set my thoughts on my course work.

The size of the university, in itself, frightened me. Recently, they had begun construction and the grounds were dug up on all sections of the university. The area was not pleasant to look at. Its academic standards were the roughest in the state, which added more terror. But, after my midterms, I was able to relax when I pulled all B's on my tests. It was my first victory over this huge megalopolis. A sense of confidence permeated my life and I realized that I was as intelligent as anyone around me. I was not a loser!

My victories were short-lived, as I learned at the end of the semester that my scholarship had been cut. I had not expected this turn of events and hadn't planned on having to find another source of money. I could get a loan, but it would take three months to be processed. In the meantime, I had no source of support. I had to leave.

There was no place to go but home. It was the last place in the world that I wanted to go, but I had no choice. And never before had I felt so defeated. I had stepped out in faith, believing God, and He had thwarted my plans. Or so it seemed, at the time. I fell into a terrible depression, thinking that maybe I had displeased God but not being able to figure out how.

I didn't want to turn to my father. I was twenty-two years old— and it was a little late in life to go home. Through contact with an old friend, Harriet, I found a place to live—with her parents. That was, until we found an apartment of our own. It was the only offer I had, so I grabbed it.

The first few weeks at home were spent witnessing to my friend and looking for a job. Harriet was very open to the Gospel and received Christ soon after I arrived. Finding a job was a bit more difficult, but I felt I had scored in at least one area.

I walked from store to store, applying for any position that was open. One afternoon I saw an ad in the local paper for a job that interested me—a position for a Gal Friday. I had no idea what a Gal Friday was, but I knew that I could learn. I called the number and made an appointment for an interview. The man who spoke with me was very kind and said that he looked forward to meeting with me.

"It looks like you've done a lot of things in your short lifetime," he said when I handed him my résumé. I looked him over as he spoke with me. His hair was very gray, but he seemed to have aged with dignity. "I'm looking for someone with ambition. But, I also need a gal who will work for me for at least a year. Are you engaged?" he asked.

"No," I answered.

"Are you planning on staying around here? I know that this town doesn't offer much to young people. And most of them leave after a while. What are your plans?" he asked.

"Well, I have nowhere to go and no money to go anywhere. So, I guess this is where I'll stay," I answered.

"I have five more people to interview," he said. "I'll call you in a day or so and let you know either way. But, your application looks good," he added.

Riding home, I prayed that he would hire me. It was important to get money together quickly so Harriet and I could get our own apartment. I wanted more than anything else to be on my own again. I hated depending on anyone for help.

The next day I received a call. The job was mine! I was on my way to freedom.

Harriet also found a job that week, working for a local vet. After work we rode around town looking for apartments for rent. Eventually, we found one through another ad in the local paper—a large studio over the laundromat, smack in the center of town.

When we first moved in, Harriet took a great deal of her time to redecorate and paint. Through friends, we found enough furniture for the place and slowly it became home. But, I did not feel like I was "home." I didn't want to stay in that town any longer than I had to. There was no doubt in my mind that I was not going to put down roots. I was waiting for my escape, but tried to get myself into a routine until my day of release came.

The organization I worked for turned out to be a mail-order house. And my boss, after discovering my flare for writing, started to give me assignments for new copy for the catalog. Often he would call me into his office to discuss my work.

"Judy, look at this penny. If you were going to try to sell it to someone, what would you write about it? What would make it sell? What is unique about it? What stands out?" he asked.

I looked at him, trying to come up with some answers. But, I was baffled. "Where did you learn so much?" I asked him.

"I worked in advertising most of my life. I started as a mail clerk and when I left I was a vice-president of one of the largest advertising agencies in the world," he said.

"I think I would like to work in advertising someday," I said. "When I was a kid my dream was to be an account executive."

"Well, that would take a lot of work," he said. "If you stay here for a while and learn all that you can, it might give you a foot in the door. But you'd have to go to New York City. That's where the good agencies are," he added.

He looked at me, noticing the fear on my face. "Judy, you're a good copywriter. Better than most people who have been working at it for years. Copywriting is a skill that few people can use well. I've seen the best and I've seen the worst. If you work at it, you could be one of the best," he added.

I was amazed at his confidence in me.

"I guess you would know," I said. "But how hard is it to get into the field?"

"The competition is rough. Everyone wants to be a writer. Since you're a woman, you'd have to start as a secretary. There's no other way," he said.

"That's not too encouraging," I said. "I could be stuck at a desk shuffling papers for years. What if I never get a break?"

"That's the chance you take," he said. "But, if you want to be an account executive badly enough, you'll take it."

I thanked him for his encouragement and we continued to talk about selling that penny. "Look at how the print on it stands out," he said. "That is unique. . . ." But my mind wandered to other things.

His words started a new process in my life. My dream was coming alive again, although it had been buried for years. He was convinced that I could make it. I myself did not have that confidence, but he knew the industry. He had even mentioned giving me a recommendation for his old firm. The idea—an account executive—seemed so farfetched and unattainable. But in my mind it was closer than it had ever been.

I set my heart on moving to New York. I dreamed about it, thought it, and lived it. I was leaving! But I didn't know how to go about getting there. And I didn't have the courage to go. So for many months I prayed that God would either confirm or contradict my convictions. And I asked Him to give me the guts to step out—once again.

While I was at work one day, I felt the prodding of the Holy Spirit in my heart. Often, when God wanted to speak to me about something specific, He would nudge me all day and make me restless enough to sit down and spend a good amount of time in prayer. So that afternoon I rushed home from work and sat in my "prayer chair," waiting for God to speak.

As I prayed and opened my heart to God's voice, I saw a vision in my mind's eye. Before me was a city, covered with a dark, penetrating cloud. Above the cloud were demons pushing it down. As the picture moved in closer I saw that dark filth was seeping into the windows and homes of everyone in the city. "Oh God," I asked, "what are you trying to tell me?"

"The city," He said, "is New York. The cloud is the sin of the people. The demons are the oppressive forces working against my Church. The sin," He said, "is even in the homes of *my* people."

"That's wonderful," I thought. "But, what am I supposed to do about it?" And without His answer, I knew that God was confirming my decision to move to New York. There was something that He wanted me to do there.

After I had worked for the mail-order firm for nine months, I was writing all the copy for their catalog. I also handled their magazine editorials and local advertising. It seemed that God was preparing me—giving me some background—to break into the field of advertising. I tried to absorb all that I could until there was nothing left to learn. And then I knew that it was time to venture to New York.

I had saved a little money. And I decided to take a few days off from work and make my trip north. Just to check it out! I wanted to see the city for myself, experience the people and the environment. And it was important to know if my heart was really in this move. It was easy to dream, especially when I was so miserable where I was. The grass always looked greener on the other side of the fence. I wanted to know if it really was.

One Thursday afternoon I packed my bags and left. It was early in December and I was excited to think that I would see the Christmas lights and decorations. I had never seen them before. There was so much to do and see, and I planned my sight-seeing carefully.

Upon arrival, I checked into a small YWCA and then headed to Midtown to see the sights. Stopping along the way, I asked people for directions. The city was huge and I felt lost as I walked the crowded streets. Never in my life had I felt so small. Walking up Fifth Avenue, I stopped at Rockefeller Center and St. Patrick's Cathedral. I walked farther north to Central Park. And then I cut across and headed for Lincoln Center. But I was awestruck by the size and pace of New York. It was like nothing I'd ever experienced before. My eyes bugged out as I looked up to see the top of the skyscrapers.

After roaming around Lincoln Center, I decided to walk back to the Y. In my travels, I found Broadway and thought it would be a nice area to walk down. I knew that Times Square was somewhere near, and as I walked south, I hoped I could find it.

The Fifties approached and Times Square loomed in the background. My heart fell to my stomach. The porno theaters lined the streets. XXX-rated movies were advertised everywhere. Massage parlors vied for customers. Prostitutes, hustlers, and derelicts lined the streets. And tourists and local sightseers made their way through the crowds. I was appalled. I had no idea that such a filthy, decadent place thrived. I hopped on a bus, and closed my eyes as I finished my trip through the area.

All during the weekend, I walked and bused around the city. The Upper East Side and the West Side impressed me. Midtown was too congested. Downtown was too dirty. Most of all I liked the East Side. It seemed calm and safe. I wanted to get a feel for the city so I'd know what I was getting into if I moved there. And during my travels I came across a Christian community, right in the center of a residential area.

"New York Christian Community" the plaque said on the

front. I stood and looked at the large brownstone before I entered. It seemed so odd to me that a group of Christians had found a house and congregated together. Curious, I walked inside.

A receptionist greeted me as I entered. "I'm not from New York but I noticed your sign as I was walking past. What's this place all about?" I asked.

"Well," the woman answered, "we were a group of Christians who found it very difficult to survive alone in the city. So, we got together and rented this building. There are about thirty of us living here now. We have Bible study, times of sharing and a service on Sunday. Are you interested in living here?"

"Well, I'm thinking of moving to New York and I'd need a place to stay," I said. "I'm from West Virginia and I'm here looking over the city."

"Well, let me call the director," she said. "He could give you an application to fill out and show you around. Sometimes we have a room open. He could put you on the list," she added.

I smiled as she dialed the director's office. And I sat on a chair biting my fingernails as I waited for him to come down.

"Hi, my name is Bob Harris," he said. "I am the director of this place and I hear that you'd be interested in living here."

"I told your receptionist that I might be moving to New York. And as of now, I don't have a place to live," I said.

"Fill out this application, and when you're done, I'll show you around. We're not that big, but we like to think we're a family," he added.

I filled out the application and answered questions that included everything from my religious beliefs to personal habits. When I finished, Bob took the form and led the way around the building.

First he showed me the residence. People had to double up in rooms because there weren't enough for everyone to have a single. The guys had a floor and so did the girls. The rooms were small, but they looked cheerful and comfortable. We walked upstairs to the small chapel and administrative offices.

"This is where we have service on Sunday," Bob said. "If you come, we'd like you to join us. And over here are the offices of those of us who run this place." We walked around and then started downstairs, covering the living room, kitchen, and recreation room.

"I think it might be nice to live here," I said. "How much rent do you charge?" I asked.

"Well, it's a hundred and fifty dollars a month. That covers maintenance. Food is extra. We put in fifteen dollars a week apiece and try to eat together. It doesn't always work out that way because people have different schedules. If you wanted to do your own cooking, that would be fine," he said.

"When could I come?" I asked him.

"We'll have a vacancy in a month. In the meantime, I'll go over your application and let you know if we can take you." As he talked, I noticed how peaceful the building was—a far cry from the streets of New York. The people who passed by us as we walked through the building were friendly. Most of them were my age or a little older. They made me feel welcome.

"Well, here's my phone number," I said. "Call me when you have decided if I can come or not."

I walked out of the building and the cold winter air hit my face. The love and peace of God, which I had felt so intensely in the community evaporated in the air. I was alone again and I didn't know a soul. As I walked down the street, I wondered if I was crazy to think that God wanted me to come to New York City. I decided to put it out of my mind when I got home. The whole idea was preposterous.

When I got back home, I was anxious and undecided about what to do. "I need time to think it through," I told myself. "God will make it clear to me."

Monday I returned to work, trying to get back into the dull routine. I was so bored with work, so sick of living in a small tourist town that was dead three quarters of the year. "This is no way to live," I thought, as I sat at my desk to start my day's work.

"Did you see the sights?" my boss asked me as he walked into my office. "Some town, huh?"

"Yeah, I saw a lot. But the place is so big. And I don't know anyone. How will I ever find a job?" I asked.

"Oh, you'll meet people and make contacts," he said, smiling confidently. "There are ways. When you move there, find an employment agency and try for a job as a secretary at an agency. And then have the patience to wait for your promotion."

I listened to his words, but I was not thoroughly convinced that I had a lot of time to waste as a secretary. Never had I done things the conventional or accepted way. God always opened a door and made a way before me.

I prayed during the next weeks about moving to New York. I felt that God was telling me to go and also to live in the Christian community. And that disturbed me.

"Oh, come on, God," I said. "You know as well as I do how bad Christian communities can be. Why do you want me to live in one? I had enough of that in the past. Can't I just get my own place?" I asked.

I sat listening for an answer. I thought that maybe if I bugged God long enough He'd change His mind. We were on good terms and possibly I could twist His arm. But, He would have no part of my foolishness and waited for me to change my mind.

"Call the community," a still voice within said to me. "Call and see if you have been accepted."

Reluctantly, I picked up the phone and dialed the number, hoping the director would be away. But, he picked up the phone in his cheerful manner.

"Hi, Judy, I was just thinking of calling you. We have accepted your application and you can move in any time now."

"Well, I don't know when I'd be coming. There are a lot of loose ends to tie up here. Can I call you when I'm ready to move?" I asked.

"Sure! We'll hold the room for you. I think you'd be a positive addition to our community. Let me know. . . ."

But, I was still convinced that God was making the wrong decision. I continued to pray, hoping I'd get a different answer. But, the same thought kept coming to my mind. "GO!!" I could resist no longer.

The next day I gave notice at work. "Judy, I think you're doing a good thing by going. You've been here a year now and you've done well. If you need a reference, I'd be happy to give you one," my boss said.

That evening I began to pack. My roommate was sad to see me

go. "If this is what you want, you should do it. You're not much of a country person anyway. You'll like the city life," she said.

"Yeah, but I have to start all over again. I don't know anyone there. I don't have a job. God is going to have to do a big miracle for me. And, I guess that's good. . . ." I mumbled as I stuffed things in boxes.

But, as much as I was complaining, I was really excited. New York City!! That was the big time. "I'm going to New York to be an executive," I told myself. "I hope it doesn't take long."

The morning of my departure I was both sad and happy. I called my family to say good-bye and checked around the apartment for anything I might have left behind.

Convinced that I had everything, I began my trip to the post office, mailing what I could not take on the train. Harriet helped me get the rest of my things in her car. And we headed for the train station.

"Do you think I'm crazy for doing this?" I asked her as we drove along. "I have only fifty dollars to my name. I don't have a job. I don't know anyone. Isn't it a little crazy to do something like this?"

"Not if you're obeying God," she answered. "He won't let you down. You'll see."

We pulled up at the train station and I pulled my suitcases out of the car. "Harriet," I said. "I don't think I'll ever come back here. There's nothing left for me. This place was a neat area to grow up in, but it's no place to settle down. Will you pray for me?" I asked.

"Sure I will. You just keep the faith," she said.

I stepped on the train, took care of my luggage, and sat down in an empty seat.

"My friends at Willis would never believe this," I said to myself. "They probably think I'm locked up in some loony bin."

I looked out the window and watched the town fade behind me. "Good-bye old life—hello New York!!"

12 And He Will Give You the Desires of Your Heart

When I entered Penn Station I called the community, asking the receptionist if she could send someone to help me with my things.

"Grab a Red Cap and get a taxi," she said. "It won't take you more than fifteen minutes to get here."

"O.k.," I said, checking to make sure I had the address right. "I'll see you real soon."

When I entered the brownstone, a woman whom I had not seen before offered to help me with my bags. I was grateful.

"My name is Kris," she said. "I've been living here for about two months now. I know what it's like to need help with your stuff. When I moved in I needed an army to carry my things."

"My name is Judy," I replied. "I just arrived from West Virginia."

"Well, if you're new, you're bound to meet lots of Christians in this place. People come and go all the time," she said. "What do you do—for work I mean?"

"I'm a copywriter—of sorts. I've done some writing and editing. Nothing to brag about. I want to find a job in advertising."

"I'm sure that God will help you," she said. "Here's your room," she said, pointing to a room at the end of the hall. "It overlooks the street. That's a treat around here. Most of the rooms look out on brick walls."

"This must be my lucky day!" I exclaimed. "I really appreciate your help. Are you around here much?"

"I live down the hall in room 403. I travel a lot and don't stay around too much. But, I'll see you again," she added.

"O.k., see you. Thanks again!"

I turned around to look at my room. The walls were light blue and the trim a dark blue. It was a fair size, as rooms go. The ceilings were so high that it made the room look larger. I walked to the closet and opened it. Half was filled with the clothes of my roommate—who had yet to show her face. I unpacked and walked down the hall and picked up the intercom.

"Hi, this is Judy on the fourth floor. I'm expecting some packages. They probably won't come for a week or so. But, when they arrive, will you let me know?" I asked.

"Sure," the receptionist answered. "What room are you in?"

"I'm in 401. Is the director around?"

"Yes. Let me connect you."

"Can you do that on this phone?" I asked.

"Sure can. That's why they put them in," she answered.

I waited for the director to answer and then asked if I could talk with him about my rent. He told me to come right to his office so we could talk.

"I came here on faith," I said. "That means I only have fifty dollars to my name. I can give you thirty dollars for the first week's rent. I need the rest for food. I want to cook for myself, because I don't know what my schedule will be. Is that all right?" I asked.

"Sure," he said. "I made you a list of your chores. You'll be responsible for sweeping the halls and cleaning the ladies' bathroom once a week. Is that o.k.?"

"That's fine with me," I answered. "I have to go now. Is there anything else I should know?"

"Well, not really. Everyone comes and goes as they please around here. On Tuesday night we have Bible study at seven o'clock. Sunday service is at eleven o'clock. We'd like you to join us," he said.

"I'll come see what it's like," I answered. "But I can't make a commitment right now. I have a lot of things to work out."

"I understand. I'll see you soon," he said.

I said good-bye and ran to my room to get my coat. There was food shopping to do and I also wanted to look over my neighborhood. Outside, the raw winter air hit my face. Everything around me looked so big and so new. I was overwhelmed.

The next few days I met many of the people who lived in the community. It was hard to remember the names and then place them with the faces. Everyone was going in a different direction and there was seldom time to talk with anyone beyond a nice hello. Even my roommate, Carol, was seldom home. She worked odd shifts at a restaurant. But I was thankful for the time alone.

After being there for five days, I knew it was time to look for a job.

I showered and dressed and, not knowing where to start, turned south and headed for Midtown.

"Are you going to do a miracle?" I asked God as I walked down the street. "Wait on me and trust my leading," He said.

"O.k.," I answered. "You're the boss. I have to trust you because I sure don't know what I'm doing."

I walked on, turning west through the early-morning rush-hour crowd. People dashed past me, all in different directions. I felt smothered and pushed. Stepping up my pace, I turned west on Forty-third Street.

Walking into the building of a well-known large New York corporation, I was stopped by a guard and directed to a reception desk.

"I want to go to personnel," I said.

The guard handed me a pass marked "temporary" and pointed to the elevators. "Turn in the pass on your way out," he said.

I could not believe that I was actually in such a prestigious place. This was a miracle way beyond my belief. I stared at the other people in the elevator with me, wondering if they were famous. "You have real good taste," I said to God as the elevator rose. "Nothing like taking me right to the top." At my floor, I walked off and searched for the personnel office.

A receptionist greeted me and handed me an application form. "Fill this out and then someone will call your name. It won't be long." I took a seat and began the process of filling in the blanks.

A young woman stepped out of a cubicle and called my name. I stood and followed her back to her office. "I want you to take a typing test," she said. "I might have a job for you, but you have to type well. We've had a hiring freeze for sixteen months, but we do take on part-time temporary help during the busy season. Follow me," she added as she walked me to a small office with a typewriter.

I sat and practiced for a few moments and then she returned to time me. I scored eighty-nine words per minute with no errors. She smiled as she wrote the score at the top of the test.

"We need help in the advertising department. You can start on Friday. We'll take a week to train you and then you go to work."

"That's fine," I said as I rose to leave.

"Oh, by the way, the job pays eight dollars and fifty cents an hour. And you'll be working about thirty hours a week."

I looked at her as though she were crazy. "Eight dollars and fifty cents an hour?" I asked.

"Yes," she said. "And if you decide to stay on, you'll get a raise in six months. Is that o.k.?"

"Fine," I answered. "It's just fine."

I took the elevator downstairs and turned in my pass at the security desk. Then I walked back out into the brisk winter air. The wind was whipping down Broadway and I pulled my coat close to my body. I was in a daze from what had just happened.

"You certainly did a miracle today," I said to God as I walked down the street. "How'd you get so good at this?" I asked, looking in the store windows as I moved on.

"I've been in the business for a long time," he said to me. "Does what I can do surprise you?" He asked.

"Not really," I said. "I just don't see miracles like that too often."

Work began on Friday and my new life fell into a routine after a while. The work was demanding and exhausting and I often returned home dead on my feet. At times like that I went straight to my room and collapsed on my bed. But, on days when I was not so worn out, I spent time with the people I lived with.

New York Christians, at least those I met, were a completely different breed of people from those I had ever known. They were energetic and involved in the world around them—always in a hurry to rush here or there. This was very hard for me to keep up with, since I was a country person at heart.

There were many differences between these people and myself. I felt as if I shared so little with them. I had been taught to live a simple life by those who had led me to Christ. But in New York, life was not that simple. It was a fast life and often brutal. I began to call my new life "life in the raw," for that's how it seemed to me. And I thought that maybe the only way to keep sane was to keep up. But, in trying to do that, I lost my peace. I decided to try another tactic—and that was to slow some of my friends down.

"Pat," I said to one of the girls I knew, "would you like to go out to lunch today? There's a nice little place around the corner that just opened."

"Well, I have so much to do today. Can we make it another time?" she asked.

"Sure," I said. "Another time."

I walked up to another girl in the community. "Sarah, do you want to go out to lunch or maybe to a movie? There's lots of good stuff playing on Broadway."

"Judy, I have work to catch up on today. How about next week?" she asked.

I walked away. It would not have been so bad if this happened once or twice. But, it was a scene that repeated itself week after week, month after month. I tried all the tactics I knew of to get involved with the people around me. On "work days" I threw myself into cleaning the community. When special events were scheduled, I offered to help. I cooked dinners for people. I suggested outings for my friends. But everywhere I turned, I was blocked from real intimacy with anyone in the community. Trapped, I decided to talk to some of my "friends" about the problem. "Pat, I think that the people around here really don't know each other. They're kind of playing a game. Everything is surfacy—but there's no real intimacy," I said.

"Judy, you're being critical. And you have no right to do that," she answered.

"I don't think so," I said. "I think I'm being honest. Christ has a way of uniting people and it doesn't happen around here. There are some real serious spiritual problems in this community."

"Stop being critical. You have no right to judge people. If you don't like the way things are around here then you'd best move out. You'll only cause division," she added.

"Does being honest constitute division?" I asked. "'Cause if that's how people around here feel, then I *should* get out. But, I think Christ was honest with people about where they were at."

"Leave me alone, Judy," she said. "I don't have time to talk about things like that." And with that, she walked away. And for the rest of the time I lived at the community, she avoided me.

I was heartbroken and all I knew to do was pray. I prayed for her and I prayed for myself. And very soon some people moved into the community who felt the very same way I did. There were just a few of us, but we all planned our escape from the community. We huddled together and shared our lives on a deeper level, knowing this trial was not forever.

My job came to an end and I did not agree to stay on. I felt that it was time to look for "my job" at an advertising agency. And one day I found an ad in the Sunday *Times* that looked perfect. Monday morning I reached for the phone and made an appointment.

I dressed carefully and added a touch of makeup. Having heard so much about the glamour of advertising, I wanted to look my best and make a good impression.

While waiting for my interview, I noticed that the agency was not too large and most of the employees were in their thirties. My palms began to sweat from the tension I felt.

A young woman called me in for the interview and we sat in the conference room. She began to talk about the industry, reminding me of the constant pressure and long hours. And then she moved on to the job.

"You'd work for me. I have a tremendous volume of work processed through my office every day. You'll have to learn deadlines all across the country and also how to set up ads. The rest is pretty easy to learn."

I studied her as she spoke to me. She wore a silk blouse and a suede skirt. A scarf was tied around her neck and her hair was perfectly styled. I had never seen such a well-dressed woman in all my life. She dressed beautifully but subtly.

After looking over my résumé, she told me that she had four girls to see after me. "But, I'll call you tomorrow one way or the other." I thanked her for her time and left.

So many questions ran through my mind as I walked home. I was a country person. Could I take the pressure? Would I be able to learn all the details of the industry? Was this what I really wanted?

But, the next afternoon, my interviewer called me and offered me the job. "We need you to start tomorrow. It's our busiest day and I need the help desperately. Do you want the job?" she asked.

All doubts flew from my mind and I immediately said yes. I hung up the phone, praising God for opening this door for me.

When I arrived the next morning, a half hour early, Sally briefed me on the job. "You might be backed up for hours at a time, but there are girls around who can help you." She showed me how to set up display and classified ads and pulled out her files to familiarize me with her accounts. "Just follow everything the way it is. Most clients repeat ads week after week."

"Thanks for the help," I said. "It will take me a while to get used to this. It's all so new."

"Would you be interested in doing sales someday?" she asked me. "I started out in sales seven years ago and now I work for myself. The money is really in being an account executive," she added.

"That's what I always wanted to do," I exclaimed. "That's my dream."

"Well, tell you what. You work hard for a year. Learn the industry. And at the end of that time, I'll see that you get into sales."

"Really?" I said. "Is it that easy?"

"If you have the disposition for it. We could always use another account exec around here. I think you have the personality for it. We'll talk about it in the future. You have enough to think about right now," she added.

Time on the job flew and after a few months I could not believe that I'd been there so long. I was always under pressure and had little time to stop and rest. I liked the excitement of the industry, but I hated the long, draining hours.

"It's the price you have to pay if you want to be a success," Sally reminded me one day. "Pay the price and then you get the rewards," she added.

"Yeah," I said. "But, while I'm paying the price, I have little time left to do anything else. I'm too exhausted."

"This is a career job, Judy. If you don't want a career, you don't belong here."

"I guess so," I said, wondering how long I would have to pay my dues.

After I had established myself with the agency, I found a Christian woman named Terry who was looking for a roommate. She had previously lived in the community and knew me from there. I rushed to her place after work to talk about the details, hoping this was God's "escape" for me. After only an hour of talking, we decided that we would like to live together. I moved in the next weekend.

That summer was the hottest and most oppressive I ever spent. It was also a time of great tension in New York, since Son of Sam, the notorious psychotic killer, was on the loose and the FALN was bombing large corporation headquarters in the area. To top it all off, there was the blackout of '77 which paralyzed the whole city. I had never been through something like that and began to pray about leaving the City. But God confirmed over and over again that He wanted me there. And He promised to protect me.

During this time I met a man who began to ask me out. At first, I agreed to go out for coffee or shopping. But, one evening he invited me to his apartment for dinner. I was not sure about going. I was a little shaken by the events of the summer and was not finding it easy to trust strangers.

But, he talked to me about his job and began to open up about his life. I told him that I was not in the market to get emotionally involved and he agreed to keep his distance.

He cooked a lovely roast and sat over dinner telling me about his work as an accountant. I listened and shared my dreams of becoming an account executive. Lately I had been writing copy for many of the account execs I worked with and this was a great source of pride for me. He listened intently.

After dinner, he walked out of the room for a moment. "Come on back here," he said. "I want you to see the view of the city."

"O.k.," I said. "But just for a moment." I stood up and walked to the rear of the apartment, following his voice. Then I saw that he was standing in his bedroom. I hesitated as I walked in, but he was pointing to the beautiful view from his window.

"That's really nice," I said. "Not many people can afford that kind of view. Let's go back in the dining room and finish our conversation," I said, trying to lead him out the door.

"Not so fast," he said, as he turned and stared at me, from feet to head.

I looked into his eyes and knew that he had other things on his mind. As I started to walk away, he grabbed my arm and wouldn't let me go. I searched his face again, hoping that he was joking with me. A second look said that he was not. I gave him a pleading look. But it didn't help.

Suddenly he threw me down on his bed. I tried to scream, but no sound came out of my mouth. As he started to tear off my clothes, I struggled and fought, but to no avail. The more I fought the more encouraged he was to keep tearing.

I tried to talk to him, thinking that I could talk him out of raping me. But my words came out all jumbled and made no sense. It hit me that there was nothing I could do. My whole body froze and I went into shock.

Suddenly a Scripture came to mind—"God will never give you more than you can take, but with it will give a way of escape." I started praying. But all I could say was, "HELP!!" And every part of me screamed out that word.

I wondered if I was going to make it out alive. "If this man is crazy enough to rape me, he might just kill me," I thought. "Spare my life, God," I said. "I'll do anything you want if you just spare me."

Finished with me, Alfred quickly jumped up. He walked to the window and stared out. I lay there frozen with fear, when God spoke to me.

"Grab your clothes and get out of here," He said. "That man

cannot move or talk right now. I've paralyzed him. Get out quickly."

I jumped up and pulled on my clothes. Alfred stood and stared at me as I dressed. I avoided his eyes and made my way to the living room. My coat and pocketbook were waiting for me on a chair. Grabbing them, I ran to the door.

"Don't leave," he said to me as I touched the doorknob. He was standing across the room looking at me. "Please stay."

"You just raped me," I screamed. "Don't you know what you did? You're a sick person," I yelled as I ran into the hall and pressed the elevator button. He stood by his door, watching me as I entered the elevator.

"He doesn't know what he did," God said to me as I rode down. "He needs a lot of help. Pray for him."

As I entered the street I noticed that I had put my blouse on inside out. I pulled my coat next to my body and walked to a bus stop. Getting on, I ran to the back of the bus and sat in a corner by myself. I hung my head and cried. I was angry and shocked. "Why me, God?" I screamed inside. "WHY ME??"

The next few days are but a blur in my mind—police reports, hospital exams, visits from a detective, the feeling that bugs were crawling all over my body. But mostly all I felt was a paralyzing fear that swept through my life.

There was no sleep at night. And if I did doze off, I had nightmares about the rape. Often I would get up in the morning, walk into the kitchen and start throwing dishes around.

"Are you o.k.?" Terry asked me. "You don't look so good."

"I'M ALL RIGHT!" I screamed. "Just get away from me. Don't touch me. Don't come near me. Keep your distance."

"I'm not going to hurt you, Judy," she said. "I want to help you."

"Then make the whole world go away," I said. "Make it disappear."

"I can't do that, Judy. Maybe you should go for counseling."

"No, just let me die. Do you know that I died? I'm not alive anymore. Not really."

"Do you want to talk about it?" she asked. "You really need to."

"No, just leave me alone."

A black cloud came over my life. I wondered if Alfred was going to come and kill me. I was afraid to walk the streets of New York, so I started taking taxis wherever I went—to work, shopping, back from work, and to church. The rest of the time I sat in the house, rocking in the chair in the living room. And then I became sick.

It started as stabbing pains in my lower abdomen. And then my stomach began to ache. One night I woke up, feeling as if my stomach was turning inside out. "Terry!" I yelled from my room. "I think I'm having a heart attack. Come here!!" She ran to my room and sat on the edge of my bed.

"I can't move," I said. I described the pain. Never had I hurt so much in my whole life. I felt as if my chest was ripping apart. "Do you want me to call an ambulance?" she asked.

"No, just sit with me. If I don't feel better in an hour you can call one. But, I can't move right now."

I tried to tell her how I had been feeling. I explained my fears and nightmares. "I've been praying that God will heal me and take away this hurt. But it just doesn't go away."

"Maybe you should pray for Alfred," she suggested. "He probably needs it as much as you do."

"I hate him," I said. "I don't think I could ever forgive him."

"But, you have to if you want to feel better. That's a part of healing," she said.

The longer we talked, the less I felt the pain. "You have to get a checkup tomorrow," she said. "You can't go on like this." I closed my eyes and fell asleep after promising her that I would.

My trip to the doctor the next day proved that I had several cysts on my ovaries and the beginnings of an ulcer. "You must be under a lot of stress," he said as he handed me a prescription.

"You could never know," I said. "You wouldn't understand."

Four months after the rape, my boss offered me a job as an account executive. "You'll have to do sales and get your own clients. But, I think you'll do well," he added. I thanked him for the job and went back to my office. I knew that I should be happy, but I didn't feel as though I was moving up in the world. I felt I'd just been offered a step down.

"Terry," I said to my roommate when I got home from work, "I don't think this is the life for me. I'm working for something that has no meaning to me. Maybe I'll make thirty thousand dollars in the next year or two. But what will I have? No time for myself. No friends, no peace, and no joy."

"But, Judy," she said, "this is what you've always wanted, isn't it?"

"I thought so. But you know, sometimes I wonder if I'll be alive tomorrow. If I die tonight, what have I done? What have I contributed to the world? What have I done for God? Don't you see? Everything that I am doing is just for me. I have no time for anyone, no love left for anyone. My whole life is so selfish. I don't like it."

"Well, try out the job for a while. You can always leave," she said.

"To do what? All I know is advertising. And I hate the business world. I hate the formalities. I hate the lying and the cheating. I can't stand it."

"What else would you like to do?" she asked.

"I don't know. But, you know what? I realized the other day that I am very angry at Christians. I really don't like them," I said. "I've seen so much judgment and surfacy politeness. But God has been telling me that I *must* forgive Christians, and love them. My greatest weakness right now is my inability to accept and love people the way Christ does. I know this is wrong, but I don't know if I can change. I don't know where to begin."

"Why don't you start with forgiving yourself. At least you recognize that you don't like them. That's a start. But, I think that when you start loving yourself the way you are, you'll stop looking at Christians. They aren't going to change. Or at least you can't change them. So, change yourself," she added.

"I've never fit into Christian circles," I said. "I've always felt that I have to compromise when I get around Christians—and be someone that I'm not. And I've done it for years. I've never honestly been who I am. And I don't think God likes that," I said.

"Well, no better time to change than now," she said.

"You're right, but I have an awful lot to change. I have a lot of forgiving to do. But, if God wants me to do that, He'll have to help me," I added as I walked out of the room.

I started my new job as an account executive the next day. And try as I may, I could not make myself like it. I pretended to be happy and I pretended to be thrilled by my new position in life. But, I hated the job with all my heart. What I had always wanted seemed to melt before my eyes. I hated being stuck in an office and in an industry that made me feel sick. More than anything else, I wanted out.

"What do you really want?" God asked me day after day as I sat at my desk and solicited clients. "What do you want?" These words penetrated my life until finally I could admit my heart's desires.

"I want to write," I said to God. "And I want to minister to women with emotional problems. Those are the only two things that really turn me on. I don't want anything else."

"I will give those things to you," He said. "But, it's not time yet."

"When will it be time?" I asked Him.

"When I tell you to leave this job," He answered.

I put my mind to my work, trying to do the best job I could. When I had spare moments, I read Scripture and shut my door to pray. Little by little, I was able to let go of my anger at the church.

I began to see Christians as people very much like myself—weak, fallible, fragile, and precious in the sight of God. I became less angry with myself for not liking them and slowly, over a matter of months, I started to feel love for my brothers and sisters.

All the while, my stomach and cyst problems became worse. The longer I worked as an account exec, the sicker I became. My medication did not help and I missed many days of work. Finally, I demanded that God give me deliverance and guidance for my life. And He answered.

One day I was sitting at work, crying with frustration over all the papers on my desk. I had been sick for eight months, had missed thirty days of work, and was worn thin. I had no strength to go on and I was at the point of collapse. I knew that if I kept up like this I would end up in the hospital with nervous exhaustion.

"Leave your job," God said. "It is time to go."

"Really? Are you serious? I can leave?"

"Yes," He said emphatically.

I stood up and wiped the tears off my cheeks. And I headed to my boss's office.

Steven took one look at me when I walked in, and knew what I was going to say. He sat back in his chair, and waited for me to get it out. "You know I haven't been happy," I said. "This isn't where I belong and the sooner I get out the better. I had to try it to know if it was what I really wanted, but I can't take it, so I'm leaving."

"Judy, I like you; you've done well. Any time you want a job, you can come back and work for me. But I know you have to go, so I won't talk you out of it. Remember there will always be a position for you here," he said.

"Thanks," I answered. "You've been good to me but I just can't stay. I've got to find something better."

"Hope you do," he said skeptically.

"Good luck," he yelled as I headed for the elevator. I turned around and waved. He had tried so hard to be my friend and to help me become successful. He had so many hopes for me. And I felt guilty for having blown them.

I walked home and waited for my roommate. When she came in she was startled. "Is everything all right?" she asked. "You're home so early."

"I quit my job today," I said.

"You did?" she asked.

"Uh huh, I'm finally free."

"What are you going to do?" she asked.

"Well, remember how I've talked about writing a book," I said. "And starting a ministry for emotionally disturbed women?"

"Yeah," she answered.

"Well, that's what I'm going to do," I said.

"But what will you do for money?" she asked. "You still have bills to pay."

"I don't know," I said. "But if I follow Jesus, He will provide something."

"I don't understand you at all. You can't just drop everything all of a sudden. That's crazy."

"Not when you walk with Jesus," I answered. "He has a way of opening the toughest doors. And I believe that He'll open doors for me."

"How's He going to do that?" she asked.

"I don't know. But I know that He will. Will you join me in the ministry?" I asked.

"Are you kidding?" she asked. "I wouldn't miss it for anything in the world."

13 The Christ Advantage

I have often wondered if all the work that I put into my healing
has paid off. Particularly during times when I am struggling with a
problem or weak area of my life. Some mornings I wake up and
the same questions I had seven years ago are floating through my
head. I get discouraged. This is perhaps due to the fact that I had
once hoped that after I'd fought my way through schizophrenia I
would no longer have to struggle in life.

I have found the opposite to be true. My real problems did not
begin until after God had healed me. Up to that point I was daily
fighting for my sanity and life. Afterward I had to struggle to
maintain all that I had gained. For many years when I would
enter a difficult transition period and feel the same old feelings
(guilt, fear, frustration, and anger) I would wonder if I had
regressed. That fear stood over me for a long time. I have only
recently been able to laugh at it.

Being "saved" once meant to me that I was exempt from the
constant battle in the world around me—ego poised against ego,
power against power. I no longer felt compelled to take a position
in the battle and felt relieved to be safe from the storm.

To some degree, that was true. I discovered, however, that there
was a battle raging within me—my emotions (many of them very
old) and desires always positioned against my faith and what I
know to be true. The saddest part was that I learned I was accus-

tomed to doing things that were bad for me and tended only to be hurtful. After God had spent so much time in making me an alive and vibrant person he then turned around and asked me to "die to self." What He meant was that I should let go of those things in my life which hurt me—my fears, anger, bitterness, etc.

But after my healing, I presumptuously believed that God had completed the deepest work in my life. I felt secure that I was now free from those lonely, soul-searching times when my food was my tears and my joy was the coming of Christ to set me free. During the summer of '74 I was on a mountaintop, flying free from a past which had tormented me. I looked forward to a fulfilling, peaceful life. I believed it would be easier than what I'd been through.

I was totally wrong in believing that I had "made it." I had made it through one stage of life, only to be walking toward another. Where most people come to Christ with some semblance of sanity in their lives, I had come as an empty, shattered shell. So, during the summer of '74 I had reached the place where most people are when they find Christ. And the past four years have been full of steep hills, plateaus, green fields, and valleys. All of it very much the cycle of life and the life of a Christian.

Although I had won the battle over a tormenting disease, I had little experience in facing life victoriously on a day-to-day basis. The years following my recovery were the proving ground of my healing and my salvation. And there have been times when I've wanted to give up.

It is enough, I have often thought, that we have to face life and overcome the battles we enter. Yet I have had to live in two worlds, my past and my present. The past never goes away. You learn to accept it but you don't ever forget it. It is easiest to remember when you are struggling in the present, almost impossible to put out of mind. When things become rough in the present, I often look back and remind myself of all that God has brought me through.

How do you deal with pain and suffering? Does it get easier? I think not. I don't think the human body was built to hold a lot of pain, for at some point it will begin to break down under the stress. If life is always to be full of stress and strain, and if we, as

Christians, must endure, I have had to repeatedly ask myself, "What is the Christ Advantage?"

One such time was during the summer of 1977. My rape made me question every value I had, every belief I held to be true, my sense of security and my own dignity as a person.

I would awake some mornings and throw things around the house. My rage was so deep, the humiliation I felt so overwhelming that I thought perhaps I had deceived myself into believing that God loved me.

But, I could look back and *know* that He was always with me, He had always (somehow) pulled me through.

One of my strengths has always been my insight. It is easy for me to "see into" a situation. God has poured His grace upon my life, perhaps knowing how much I need it—even when I don't know that I do. I have been able to understand much of the depths of my heart—and the hearts of others, because of my own lonely, soul-searching times.

But sometimes the pain you feel inside and the loneliness you experience transcend your knowledge or understanding and you are left with many emotions you must work through and overcome. Head knowledge of the sickness of a rapist does little to alleviate the trauma of a rape experience. Being told that you are angry or hurt helps little also.

And during times of great suffering, you are left very much alone to work through your pain. Scripture says that no one can know another person's joy or sorrow. This you quickly learn when you are hurting.

And so, if Christianity does not mean exemption from the often severe struggles of life, what does it mean? I may offend those who feel they are protected (by God) from the harsh realities of life. I don't address them. I speak to the majority of people who have had to fight through difficulties—especially the mentally and emotionally disturbed.

If there were no advantage to Christianity, I would long ago have rejected Christ and traveled to other circles, perhaps Freudian psychology (it would have explained my illness) or Assertiveness Training (it would have told me how to fight back). Most probably I would have worked to acquire great wealth. Instead, I have chosen to be a friend of the afflicted and oppressed, the poor and rejected. Christian prosperity is not something to be solely desired. I find it selfish to think that I should live in luxury and comfort while thousands of people (whom God loves) are living in darkness. I feel this way because of the Christ Advantage.

The Christ (or Christian) Advantage is wrapped up in one word and that is Jesus. Jesus means a lot of things to many people. To some He is a cause to promote. To others He is an escape. Some think He was the author of community life and live in that life as if that is "it." But, in traveling these circles I have often left thinking, "Has anyone seen Jesus lately?"

In non-Christian circles I have heard people say, "I don't have time to think about God." And what I think they mean is that they haven't needed God. That, I think, is a valid answer for a non-Christian. I respect it and accept it because I know and remember times when I didn't feel a need for God. Why get tangled up with someone you don't need?

The Christ Advantage is our human need for Jesus and His ability to meet our every need. Some of us have to hit rock bottom before we see that and maybe a part of the sadness of life is that we hold out so long before we reach out to God.

What I have been through has taught me how much I need God. Before my illness I was stubborn and refused help from anyone who tried to reach out to me. I was plainly tired of hearing the same old answers (you're lazy, you have committed a great sin and this is your punishment, you're irresponsible, etc.).

So, why was I ill? Because for many consecutive years of my life I had needs which were not being met. I needed, very deeply, to be loved, very gravely to give love in return. I needed to be recognized as a worthwhile person and I needed a reason to live. None of these needs were being met in a way that was personally right for me. And over a number of years I became very ill.

When I first met Christ, I was told (by church people) to read the Bible, pray, and go to church, as if this were the answer to my problems. God, in His wisdom and understanding of me, knew better and He drew very close to me.

And He would say, "Judy, I love you very much. You are very special to me. I think of you many times during the day and I am concerned about your welfare. I will get you through. I will heal you and make you whole. Hold on to me."

No one had even spoken to me before in such a manner. I had never been special to anyone—at least I'd never felt special. No one had promised to be with me forever. No one had ever told me that *they* could make me whole.

The first four years of my walk with God I was mostly intrigued by the promises He made to me. I decided early that if He were to break even one, I would leave Him. I waited for God to speak to me because His voice could still the roughest sea and ease the greatest ache. I sensed His love, but for many years I distrusted it. I had no basis of trust in my life, for love had always meant disappointment to me. I knew so little of the joy of being loved and loving in return. All I knew was that He was there and that somehow He would get me through. I had little time to think about being prosperous. I had little strength to become a vibrant member of community. All I knew was that I had Jesus—and I wasn't sure who He was. I just knew *that* He was. And that for some reason He had decided to make me well. I seemed to have no choice in the matter.

The Christ Advantage is that Jesus never changes. He remains the same. His faithfulness toward us remains unchanged. Victories, defeats, people, churches, money, prosperity, poverty, affliction, health, illness, life, and death—these things come and go like the changing of the tides. Yet Jesus remains the same.

After my healing I felt that I had the advantage over other Christians, in that I now understood things they had never thought about. I could relate (at ease) to the extremely ill people I came in contact with. I could love them. I felt I had the edge. But God turned me around and crushed this way of thinking in my life. And He said, "If you have anything, it is that you have experienced and know of my love when all else failed. You have been given hope when there was none. You have felt me cry when you cry, laugh when you laugh. The only advantage you have is that you have found me to be a very alive God who loves you very much and cares about every detail of your life."

But I wanted more than that. I wanted God to rearrange life to my liking, to reinforce my ideals and make everyone into the kind of people I wanted them to be. Instead, He helped me overcome my resistance to reality so that I could accept life as it was.

What is the Christ Advantage as compared to the many therapies and self-help strategies that are popular today? Well, I've spent many years in "the chair" and I have read just about all the books on the pop-help market today. But when I walked out of the therapist's office or put down my book, I had someone who would walk with me until my next session or my next reading. I had a person who would say, "I love you," when I needed to hear it most. I spent some lonely dark hours in the middle of the night when I could not talk with my therapist. But I could talk to Jesus. And He would talk to me.

The love, faith, and hope that I found were sent by God. My love is not wrapped up in pretty bows and sentimental feelings. It is based on the fact that God loves me and from that I can go out and live a normal life. My faith is not in some idea or theory that has been conjured up by men. My faith is in God, as He is revealed to me through the Bible and whatever revelation He gives me. My hope is not so much in a better tomorrow, or an answer to my problem. My hope is in God, that He will always be there and never leave me.

What does it mean to be "saved"—especially for the broken? I think that mainly it means to be saved from yourself. If I have one very alive enemy on this earth, it is myself. No one can hurt or destroy me the way I can. And God is saving me from myself. For me that has meant freedom. I can trust in God's wisdom for my life which has proven to be flawless. I can put my life in His hands and know that He is taking me somewhere. I can fight through the darkest hours and not give up because I know He has a reason. I know He loves me and I know He cares. And it is the only thing in this world I can depend on. Everything else changes from day to day.

If I were to look at my life and try to make sense out of the things that have happened to me I would go crazy. There is no sense to it. But God took my life and in the center of it He put Himself. When I walk the streets of New York and deal with the confusion of city life I am more deeply convinced that life without God cannot help but be harsh.

In my mind I do not understand God. I cannot make Him fit into my reasoning. I can know things about Him and understand parts of His personality. But in my heart I know His love. Sometimes when I look at a sunset or a bouquet of flowers I can't help but think that God must be very much like them—simple, pure, beautiful. It makes it easier to understand all my heart has experienced—that Jesus knows me.

I cannot help but be amazed that I still doubt, that I still wonder. Someday He will change that. But I know that no matter what happens He loves me the way I am. And this has made it worthwhile.